Our New England Ancestors and Their Descendants, 1620-1900; Historical, Genealogical, Biographical

SIGNING OF THE COMPACT   FOUNDATION OF GOVERNMENT   PERILS OF THE PILGRIMS

Our New

England Ancestors

and their

Descendants

1620 - 1900

Historical, Genealogical, Biographical

Compiled by

Henry Whittemore

Author of the Genealogical Guide to the Early Settlers
of America and other works.

New England Ancestral Publishing Co.
New York, 1900

Preface.

GREAT credit is due to the New England Society for its efforts to perpetuate and keep alive the memory of our New England ancestors, but it is a duty equally incumbent on those of the present generation to preserve in permanent form for the use of posterity the genealogical records and personal achievements of our ancestors, and to show what part each generation bore in the construction and defense of our Colonies and later of our American Republic

The design of the present work is to afford all who are so disposed to preserve in permanent form their line of ancestry as well as the personal achievements of their ancestors As a foundation of the work an outline history of the Plymouth Colony is given together with four generations of the Bradford and Allied Families Whether of Mayflower descent or not, every descendant of a New England family will be entitled to representation in the work, and no pains will be spared to make the record of each complete Ample space will be allowed those who are willing to bear their pro rata of the expense Illustrations of old homesteads, family portraits and relics will form an important feature of this work Each family record with all the preceding matter will be published as fast as received, and parties may procure at a moderate price as many copies as they desire.

FORMATION OF THE PILGRIM COLONY

The movement which led to the formation of the Pilgrim Church began in the Manor House at Scrooby, about 1605-6, under the ministrations of Richard Clyfton and John Robinson, and in the winter of 1607-8 an unsuccessful attempt was made by the members to reach Holland from Boston, in Lincolnshire. During the spring of 1608, they succeeded in making their escape and reached Amsterdam in safety. Among the names of those mentioned as being associated with William Bradford at this time or soon after were Elder William Brewster, William White, Isaac Allerton, Samuel Fuller, John Carver, Miles Standish, Stephen Tracy and a few others. Davis in his "Ancient Landmarks of Plymouth" says "It is fair to presume that the Pilgrim community in Leyden was made up of members representing all the different classes of English life, outside of the circles of noble families, bound together by a common religious faith regardless of those differences in education and culture and social standing, which were insignificant indeed in comparison with their real bond of union. It was doubtless this disregard of social distinctions, forced on them by the necessities of their situation, which planted in their hearts that democratic seed, which at a later day germinated and grew in the soil of New England. It was the life of labor, too, led by them in Holland, which hardened their hands for the duties and hardships of a life in the wilderness, and which developed in their natures those capacities for practical, economical and thrifty work, without which their attempt at colonization would have been a failure."

DEPARTURE FOR AMERICA.

By the 11th of June everything was in readiness. Those of the Leyden company who were going to New England had sold their estates, putting their money into the common stock; the agents of the company in England had hired the Speedwell of sixty tons, and sent her to Delfthaven, to convey the colonists to Southampton, and the Mayflower of one hundred and eighty tons, had been engaged to meet them at that place, and join her consort for the voyage. "On the 31st of July" says Bradford "they left the goodly and pleasant citie which had been their resting place near 12 years, but they knew they were pilgrimes, and looked not much on those things, but lift up their eyes to the heaven, their dearest countrie and quieted their spirits." On or about the first of August 1620, they set sail in the Speedwell from Delfthaven, and on the 15th both the Mayflower and Speedwell, with one hundred and twenty passengers on board some of whom were for the first time joining the company sailed from Southampton. On the 23rd they put into Dartmouth, with the Speedwell leaking, and on the 31st sailed again. Further disaster to the Speedwell obliged a return to Plymouth, where the Speedwell was abandoned, and eighteen passengers, including Robert Cushman, gave up the voyage. On the 16th of September, a final departure from Plymouth took place and on the 21st of November,

after a passage of sixty-six days, the Mayflower dropped anchor in Cape Cod harbor. "Like the down of the thistle they were wafted across the sea, and the seed they bore of popular government and religious freedom was planted on these western shores"

On the eleventh day of December (old style), the exploring party of Pilgrims who had left their ship, the Mayflower, in Cape Cod harbor, landed at Plymouth where they found "a place (as they supposed) fitt for the situation, at least it was ye best they could find and and ye season and their presente necessities made them glad to accept of it So they returned to their shippe again with this news to ye rest of their people, which did much comforte their harts."

On the 20th of December the Mayflower dropped her anchor in the harbor of Plymouth.

LANDING OF THE PILGRIMS.

(SEE FRONTISPIECE)

When the Pilgrims landed at Plymouth they were not only outside of the limits of their patent, on a territory of a company from which they had received no grant, but they had settled themselves where the natives of the soil might dispute their right of occupation. They exercised tact, wisdom and good judgment in their dealings with the natives and thus secured their friendship. "By the gift from Massasoit," says Davis, "the Pilgrims, without charter from the King, or patent from the Northern Virginia Company, obtained a foothold and possession, which under a charter or patent alone would have been usurpation and robbery." A patent, however, was necessary to establish their rightful claim, and the Mayflower carried the news to England of the place of their landing, as well as an application to the Northern Virginia Company, for a suitable grant. After the Pilgrims sailed from England, the Northern or Plymouth Company secured a new charter from the King, dated the 5th of November 1620

The first civil act of the Pilgrims after their arrival in Cape Cod Harbor, was to draw up a compact or "combination," as it is called by Bradford, which was signed by the male members of the company, and became the foundation on which the structure of our government has been built. Under date of Nov 21st, Mourt's Relation states that "this day, before we came to harbour, observing some not well affected to unity and concord, but gave some appearances of faction, it was thought good there should be an association and agreement, that we should combine together in one body, and to submit to such government and governor as we should, by common consent, agree to make and choose, and set our hands to this that follows, word for word."

THE MAYFLOWER COMPACT.

On the 11th day of November, 1620 (old style), there was drawn on the lid of a chest on board of the Mayflower, at Cape-Codd, and signed by forty-one of the principal men of the first band of Pilgrims, a platform of government known as the Compact, and which gave to these people the claim of being the first "Signers" of this important instrument.

The following is the full text of the Compact.

IN YE NAME OF GOD, AMEN.

We whofe names are underwritten, the loyal fubjects of our dread fovereigne Lord, King James, by ye grace of Great Brittaine, France and Ireland, King, defender of ye faith, etc , having undertaken for ye glory of God and advancement of ye Christian faith, and honour of our King and countrie, a voyage to plant ye firft Colonie in ye Northerne parts of Virginia, doe by thefe prefents folemnly, and mutualy, in ye prefence of God, and of one another, covenant and combine our felves togeather into a civil body politik for our better ordering and prefervation and furtherance of ye end aforefaid, and by vertue hearof to enacte, conftitute and frame fuch juft and equal lawes, ordinances, conftitutions and offices from time to time, as fhall be thought moft meete and convenient for ye generall good of ye Colonie, unto which we promife all due fubmiffion and obedience In witnes whereof we have hereunder fubfcribed our names at Cape-Codd ye 11 of November, in ye year of ye raigne of our fovereigne Lord, King James of England, France and Ireland, ye eighteenth, and of Scotland ye fiftie-fourth, Ano Dom, 1620

1.	JOHN CARVER	15. EDWARD TILLEY,	29 DEGORY PRIEST,
2.	WILLIAM BRADFORD,	16 JOHN TILLEY,	30. THOMAS WILLIAMS,
3	EDWARD WINSLOW,	17 FRANCIS COOKE	31 GILBERT WINSLOW.
4	WILLIAM BREWSTER,	18 THOMAS ROGERS,	32, EDMUND MARGFSON,
5	ISAAC ALLERTON,	19 THOMAS TINKER,	33 PEEER BROWN, -
6	MYLES STANDISH	20 JOHN RIGDALE,	34 RICHARD BRITTERIDGE,
7.	JOHN ALDEN,	21. EDWARD FULLER,	35 GEORGE SOULE,
8	SAMUEL FULLER,	22 JOHN TURNER,	36 RICHARD CLARKE.
9	CHRISTOPHER MARTIN,	23 FRANCIS EATON,	37 RICHARD GARDINER,
10.	WILLIAM MULLINS,	24 JAMES CHILTON,	38 JOHN ALLERTON,
11	WILLIAM WHITE,	25 JOHN CRACKSTON,	39 THOMAS ENGLISH,
12	RICHARD WARREN,	26 JOHN BILLINGTON,	40 EDWARD EOTEY,
13	JOHN HOWLAND,	27 MOSES FLETCHER,	41. EEWARD LISTER
14.	STEPHEN HOPKINS,	28 JOHN GOODMAN,	

On the same day John Carver was confirmed in the office of Governor He had already been chosen Governor on board the Mayflower, and his confirmation was doubtless a mere form rendered necessary by the adoption of a conftitution of government under which his official duties were to be performed " In the cabin of the Mayflower, then ' says Davis, " not only was the foundation stone of republican institutions on this continent laid, but the first New England town-meeting was held and the first elective officers chosen by the will of a majority." On the 27th of February the firft recorded meeting on land was held in the common house " for appointing military orders," and Miles Standish was chosen captain

THE BRADFORD FAMILY OF ENGLAND.

The name of Bradford is derived from the Saxon Bradenford or Broad-ford and is very ancient. Two towns of confiderable size in England are known by this name· one in Wiltshire, near Bath, the other in Yorkshire near Leeds.

One of the firft martyrs who perished at the stake in " Bloody Queen Mary's" term

was John Bradford, prebend of St Paul's, and a celebrated preacher   He was born at Manchester in Lancashire about 1510; was committed to prison, Aug 16, 1555, where he remained until his death   The following account is from Baker's Chronicle

" April 24, 1557, Thomas Stafford second son of Lord Stafford, with two and thirty persons (English fugitives, set on by the French King), came from France with the intention of subverting the government of the detested Queen Mary   They attacked and took Scarborough Castle, in Yorkshire, but were driven out and conquered within two days, by the Earl of Westmoreland   Stafford was beheaded on Tower Hill, May 28, 1557, and the next day Bradford and two other of his associates were executed at Tyburn

Bradford

The early, energetic, and persevering opposition to sacerdotal intolerance exhibited by Governor Bradford, the founder of the New England family of this name, would seem to indicate him as a worthy descendant of the martyr's immediate family, and that he was so is rendered more probable from the fact that the town of Bradford, in Yorkshire, Manchester, the birthplace of the martyr, and Austerfield where Gov Bradford was born thirty-three years after the martyr's death, are all in the North of England and near each other

The Bradford family have *Arms—*Argent on a fesse sable three stags' heads erased or   *Crest—*A stag's head erased or

William Bradford (1) lived at Austerfield about 1575   at which time he and John Hanson were the only subsidiaries there; Bradford being taxed on twenty shillings of land and Hanson at twenty shillings goods, annual value.   He died in 1596, leaving issue

1   William Bradford (2) who married Alice, daughter of John Hanson   He died July 12th, 1591   This William was the father of Governor William Bradford

2.   Thomas Bradford, of whom no record appears except that he had a daughter Margaret, baptized March 9, 1578

3.   Robert Bradford, baptized June 25, 1561, married Alice Wingate, Jan 3, 1585

4   Elizabeth Bradford, baptized July 16, 1570   married Janet Hill, Jan 20, 1595,
William Bradford (2) who married Alice Hanson   had

1.   Margaret, born March 3, 1585, died young

2.   Alice, born Oct 30, 1587

3.   *William*, the Pilgrim, born March, 1589.

THE BRADFORD AND ALLIED FAMILIES OF AMERICA

GOVERNOR WILLIAM BRADFORD, son of William and Alice (Hanson) Bradford, was born in Austerfield, England, March, 1588   His father died in 1591, and the infant child was then received into the home of his grandfather   the first William Bradford mentioned in this line.   After the death of the latter in 1596, he was adopted into the family of his uncle   Robert Bradford, who resided in the little village of Scrooby, two miles from Austerfield, and near the estate of the Brewsters   A church was established on the Scrooby

DEPARTURE OF THE PILGRIMS

Manor by William Brewster as early as 1606. Young Bradford was deeply impressed with the preaching of Rev. Richard Clifton and Rev John Robinson and united with the church, and was soon numbered with the "Separatists" and became a leader among them. By this course he incurred the enmity and open hostility of his relatives and neighbors. The company being threatened with persecution resolved to emigrate to Holland. In the autumn of 1607 Bradford and the other principal members of the society made an agreement with a Dutch captain to embark at Boston, but he betrayed them to the magistrates, who committed some of them to prison and sent the rest to their homes. After several months of confinement Bradford escaped in the spring of 1608, and found his companions in Amsterdam, where he apprenticed himself to a silk weaver, a French Protestant. When he came of age he sold his land in England which he inherited from his father, and engaged in business on his own account, but for lack of experience he did not succeed and met with considerable loss. Removing with the rest of the company to Leyden, about 1609, he was eager and active in promoting the scheme of emigrating to an English colony. A patent was obtained for a tract of land in Virginia with the assistance of Sir Edward Sandys, then treasurer of that colony. It was important, however, in a great undertaking of this character that he should provide himself with a 'helpmeet.' He had learned the trade of fustian or frieze weaving, " and the announcement according to custom event" was made November 15, 1613, that William Bretfoot, fustian worker, a young man from Osterfeldt, England was affianced to Dorothy May, from Wetzbutz (Wesbeach) Cambridge, England. The bans were published in Leyden, but the marriage took place elsewhere, as on Dec. 9, 1613, William Brethfoort, aged 23 years, was married to Dorothy May, aged 16 years, in Amsterdam, Holland.

On Sept 5, 1620, Bradford embarked at Southampton in the Mayflower, with the first hundred pilgrims that left for America. Obliged by stress of weather to put in at Plymouth harbor they signed a compact of government before landing according to which, John Carver, the first signer became Governor.

While engaged in the preparations for a final landing, the first great sorrow visited this little band of Pilgrims. During the absence of Bradford on one of his expeditions around the harbor of Cape Cod, his wife Dorothy fell overboard from the vessel and was drowned. After the days of mourning were over he resumed his duties and the following year Governor Carver died and on April 21, 1621, William Bradford was elected to succeed him and was continued in the office each year thereafter by the suffrage of the colonists. His authority was restricted at his own request in 1624 by a council of five and in 1633, by one of seven members. In the council he had a double vote. One of his first acts on assuming the duties of office was to send an embassy in July, 1621, to confirm the league entered into with the Indian Sachem Massasoit, the most influential and powerful of the native chiefs. His friendly relations with the Indians, who had known the English only as kidnappers were essential to the continued existence of the colony and its future prosperity. He understood the nature and character of the Indians and exhibited the combination of firmness and energy with patience and gentleness, that proved successful with the wily savage and prevented much bloodshed during the early years of the settlement. In 1622, Canonicus, Sachem of the Narragansetts, sent him a challenge in the form of a

snakeskin of arrows The Governor immediately returned the snakeskin filled with powder and shot. The sachem recognized the superiority of the pale face's equipments and immediately sued for peace

From the beginning the colonists placed implicit confidence in Governor Bradford as a leader, but owing to his precarious health William Allerton was given him as an assistant In 1623 the emigrants were reduced to famine, owing partly to the communistic system adopted at first and partly to the arrival of new comers without provisions, and Governor Bradford made several excursions among the Indians from whom he procured corn and beans and thus relieved the immediate wants of the colonists.

The fur-trading colony adjoining the Plymouth plantation in Boston harbor, provoked by their oppressions, a conspiracy among the Indians to exterminate all the English, which was revealed by Massasoit, and, on the advice of that chief, Miles Standish was sent by the Governor to put the ringleaders to death

In 1624 the English adventurers who had supplied the capital for the establishment of the colony relying on the profits of the fur-trade for their returns, were bought out, and eight of the most enterprising emigrants for a six years' monopoly of the trade assumed all the obligations of the colony.

In 1629 a patent was obtained from the New England Council—a band of English noblemen who in 1620 received from King James absolute title to the property in the colony lying between 40 and 48 degrees of north latitude—conferring upon William Bradford, his heirs and associates and assigns the title to the land on which Plymouth plantation was situated.

In 1624 the Governor and his Assistants were constituted a judicial court and afterwards the supreme tribunal of the colony, in 1629, legislation, in which up to that time all the freemen took part, was vested in a General Court to which all of the towns sent representatives, and in 1640, at the request of the General Court, Governor Bradford conveyed to it the title of the colony, reserving to himself only his proportion as a settler previously agreed upon For one period of two and one of three years he declined re-election as Governor, but was returned to the office every other year until his death He took a prominent part in all the councils which were held at his house, and in all the affairs, civil, political and military, from his house at the foot of Burial Hill, each Sabbath morning the little company of worshippers, who all assembled there, marched in procession to the place of meeting.

Governor Bradford possessed a higher degree of literary culture than was usual among persons similarly circumstanced. He had some acquaintance with Latin and Greek and also with Hebrew, was well read in history, philosophy, etc and much of his time was spent in literary work "A Diary of Occurrences" covering the first year of the colony from the landing at Cape Cod, Nov 9, 1620, till Dec. 18, 1621, was written by him in conjunction with Edward Winslow (London 1620) The manuscript of his principal work, The History of Plymouth Colony was lost for many years, but in 1846 was found in the library of the Bishop of London, at Fulham. Upon the petition of the United States Ambassador the Consistory Court of the Diocese of London, sitting at St. Paul's, March 25, 1897, ordered that the manuscript be delivered for transmission to the Commonwealth

of Massachusetts Ambassador Bayard, in whose custody it was placed, delivered it to the Governor of Massachusetts, May 26, 1897. This contains much additional and interesting data concerning the early history of the colony

Governor Bradford married 1st, Dorothy May, of Amsterdam, Holland Nov. 30, 1615 She was born in Wiesbach, England, 1597 ; drowned in Cape Cod, Dec 7, 1620. The only child of this marriage was·

John, born in Holland, married Martha, daughter of Thomas Bourne, of Marshfield, Mass., 1653, removed to Norwich, Conn and died there without issue, 1676

Governor Bradford married, 2d, Alice, daughter of Alexander Carpenter of Wrentham, England, and widow of Edward Southworth She died 1675

In his will dated May 9, 1657, Governor Bradford makes special mention of his wife as follows

" My further will is that my dear and loving wife Alice Bradford, shall be the sole executrix of my estate, and for her future maintenance my will is that my stake in the Kenebecke trade bee reserved for her comfortable subsistence as far as it will extend, and soe further in any such way as may be judged best for her "

"I further request and appoint my much beloved Christian friends, Mr Thomas Prince, Capt Thomas Willet and Lieftenant Thomas Southworth to be the suppervissors of the desposing of my estate according to the promises, confiding much in their faithfullness "

The issue of the marriage of Gov. Bradford and Alice Carpenter–Southworth was

I WILLIAM born June 17, 1624, married, 1st, Alice Richards, 1654, 2d, Widow Wiswall, 3d, widow Holmes

II MERCY, married Benjamin Vermages of Boston, June 15, 1648, lived in Plymouth

III. JOSEPH, born 1630, married Jael, daughter of Rev Peter Hobart of Hingham, Mass., May 25, 1664 He died July 10, 1715

SECOND GENERATION

JOHN BRADFORD, only child of Gov. William and Dorothy (May) Bradford no issue, did not come to this country with his parents in the Mayflower and the date of his arrival is not known. He was of Duxbury 1645, and of Marshfield, Mass 1653. He was deputy to the General Court from both places and was also a Lieutenant. He married Martha, daughter of Thomas and Martha Bourne, of Marshfield, Mass , and in 1653 removed to Norwich, Conn. He was a townsman of Norwich in 1671, but his name seldom appears on the records. His farm in Duxbury was sold by "John Bradford, gentleman " to Christopher Wadsworth in 1664 His will was exhibited at the County Court in Norwich, Conn , Sep 1676 His widow married, after a short interim, Lieut. Thomas Tracy, of Norwich John Bradford left no issue.

MAJOR WILLIAM BRADFORD,

ELDEST SON OF GOVERNOR WILLIAM BRADFORD, BY HIS SECOND WIFE MRS. ALICE SOUTH-

WORTH, NEE CARPENTER.

Major William Bradford was born June 17, 1624. He resided at Stony Brook (Kingston), probably in the same house that had belonged to his father, and the location can be easily traced at the present time. One tree of the old apple orchard that he planted was still remaining as a land mark in 1876. He was next to Miles Standish the chief military man of the colony and bore the rank of Major. In 1662 when Wamsutta or Alexander, the successor of Massasoit was suspected of designs against the English, he was with Major Winslow when the chieftain was surprised and taken prisoner. The next eventful period of his life was during 1675–6. He was chief in command of the forces from Plymouth in the great Narragansett Fort Fight when the attack was made on King Philip's stronghold. In that desperate midwinter encounter both parties fought for their very existence when nearly a thousand Indians fell a sacrifice, and of the attacking force eighty were killed and one hundred and fifty wounded. During the engagement Major Bradford received a musket ball in his flesh which he carried the remainder of his life.

He was Assistant Treasurer and Deputy Governor of Plymouth from 1682 to 1686, and from 1689 to 1691, when the colonial government terminated. He was a member of Sir Edmund Andrew's Council 1687 to 1688. He was afterwards chosen a councillor of Massachusetts. In the year 1689 he is styled by the people of Rehoboth as the Worshipful Major Bradford." It has been thought by some that this title might have been given him in connection with the Masonic Fraternity but there is no evidence of the existence of any Masonic Lodge in this country earlier than 1730–3.

Major Bradford's estate comprised the whole of the present village of Stony Brook, north of the brook, extending to the bounds of Duxbury, besides tracts of land in other parts of the town. All that portion first mentioned was bequeathed to his four younger sons, Israel, Ephraim, David and Hezekiah.

A large inheritance from his father is described on the records under date of June 1, 1663. "Whereas there was a grant by the Court of an addition of land unto Mr. William Bradford Sen. as appears upon record which was not layed out nor bounded in his lifetime; and whereas Captaine William Bradford the son of Mr. William Bradford Sen., did make request unto the Court that the same might bee performed. the Court held at Plymouth on the third of October 1662 did appoint Mr. William Collyeare and Mr. John Alden, Assistants, to view and bound an addition adjoyning unto the lands which the said William Bradford possesseth. Now wee, the above named Assistants, have this twentyeth of May 1663, viewed and bounded as followeth on the northeast from a small rundelett that runneth downe to a place commonly called the Tussukes [now called Tussock Brook] and so to range alonge northerly by Plymouth bounds next the bounds of Duxburrow and so

as to the brooke that runes into black waters to the place where the old path went to the bay. So ranging downe the brooke a mile in length."

WILLIAM COLLYARE
JOHN ALDEN

Major Bradford died Feb. 20 1701 and was buried by the side of his father on the ancient burial hill at Plymouth. On his tombstone is the following inscription.

Here Lyes the Body

of the

Honourable Major William Bradford

who

Expired February ye 20, 1703-4

aged 79 years.

He lived long, but still was doing good
And in his country's service lost much blood
After a life well spent he's now at rest
His very name and memory is blest "

"Major William Bradford in his will gives to David his house after his mother's decease: to John the land he then lived on, and also "my father's manuscripts, being a narrative of the beginning of New Plymouth, to Thomas, land in Norwich (which was his uncle John's); to Joseph, land at Norwich; to Samuel his right of commons in the Duxbury, to Israel Ephraim, David and Hezekiah, his estate, enjoining upon them to sell it to none that do not bear the name of Bradford, and be not descended from him, to Israel, a house; to David, a silver bowl, not to be alienated from the family of Bradford, to Hezekiah, a gold ring," to Samuel, his Latin books; ' to encourage him in bringing one of his sons to learning, which said books it is my will, that they shall by him be given to his said son whom he shall so bring up"

He married 1st, Alice, daughter of Thomas Richards of Weymouth.

Thomas Richards 1630, came it is supposed in the Mary and John, with sons James and John to Weymouth, Mass. He was made freeman May 13, 1640, and died soon after Dec. 17, 1650. His will, made at Hull on that day, proved Jan. 28th following, names sons John James, Samuel, Joseph and Benjamin, calling the last two minors, and daughters Mary, Ann, Alice and Hannah, the latter died 10th, Nov. following. His widow Wilthian, mother of these children, in her will of July 1679, proved November following mentions only James John and Ann, widow of Ephraim Hunt, as then living, Mary married 1st Dec. 1641, Thomas Hinckley of Barnstable, afterwards Governor of that Colony, and died June 24, 1659; Alice, married Major William Bradford (2), Deputy Governor of the same Colony.

Alice Richards the first wife of Major William Bradford died 12th Dec. 1671. He mar-

ried 2d Widow——Wiswall, married 3d Mrs Mary, widow of Rev. John Holmes, second minister of Duxbury, who died Jan. 6, 1714. She was the daughter of John Atwood of Plymouth son of Stephen Atwood and Abigail Dunham, daughter of John Dunham, of Plymouth. The Atwood homestead stood near the spot where the exploring party of the Pilgrims had their first encounter with the Indians, before landing at Plymouth.

CHILDREN OF MAJOR WILLIAM BRADFORD.

Major William Bradford by his wife Alice (Richards) Bradford had issue

I.   JOHN born Feb. 20, 1653, died Dec 8, 1736, married Feb. 5, 1674 Mercy, daughter of Joseph Warren

II   WILLIAM born March 11, 1655 died 1687, married Rebecca Bartlett of Duxbury Mass.

III.   THOMAS born about 1657, died 1708, married Anna, daughter of Nehemiah Smith of Norwich, Conn ; settled in Canterbury, Windham County, Conn.

IV.   ALICE born about 1659, died 1745; married 1st Rev William Adams of Dedham, Mass., born March 29, 1680, married 2d Major James Fitch, of Norwich, Conn

V   MERCY born 1660· married Sep 16, 1680 to Samuel Steel of Hartford, Conn.

VI.   HANNAH, born May 9, 1662, died May 28, 1738, married Nov. 28, 1682, Joshua Ripley of Hingham, Mass.

VII.   MELATIAH born about 1664, married to John Steel of Norwich, Conn

VIII SAMUEL born 1668 died April 11, 1714, married Hannah daughter of John and Elizabeth Rogers of Duxbury Mass.

IX   MARY born about 1669; married to William Hunt of Weymouth, Mass.

X.   SARAH born about 1672; married to Kenelm Baker, of Marshfield, Mass.

Major William Bradford married 2d, widow Wiswall   Their only child was

XI.   JOSEPH born 1675, died January 16, 1747: married Anna, daughter of Rev. James Fitch, of Norwich, Conn. Oct. 5. 1698; lived in Lebanon, Conn and in New London

Major William Bradford married 3d, Mary, daughter of John Atwood, and widow of Rev. John Holmes; she died June 6, 1714. They had issue

XII   ISRAEL born 1683, married Sarah Bartlett of Duxbury, daughter of Benjamin (2) son of Benjamin (1) son of Robert

XIII.   EPHRAIM born about 1685, married Feb. 13 1711, Elizabeth Bartlett.

XIV.   DAVID, born about 1690, died March 16 1730, married Elizabeth Finney or Phinney

XV.   HEZEKIAH born about 1692; died Feb. 20, 1704 married Mary Chandler of Duxbury Mass

THIRD GENERATION

LINE OF MAJOR WILLIAM BRADFORD ELDEST SON OF GOVERNOR WILLIAM BRADFORD BY HIS SECOND WIFE MRS ALICE SOUTHWORTH NEE CARPENTER

1 MAJOR JOHN BRADFORD, eldest son of Major William and Alice (Richards) Bradford, was born Feb. 20, 1653, died Dec. 8, 1736. He lived at the house, still in existence,

near the railroad at the landing. This house was partially burned by the Indians during Philip's War. The account of the affair states that "Major Bradford had removed to the guard house, and was returning in company with others to take some goods away when he discovered his house to be on fire, and saw an Indian on the brow of Abram's Hill, waving his blanket and shouting to his comrades that the white men were coming. They fled into a dense swamp by the frog pond at the base of the hill and were pursued by the Major, who fired at them, killing one as he supposed having seen him fall, but on reaching the spot was surprised at not finding the body. Subsequent events showed that the Indian was only wounded—severely—and was able to crawl behind a log of fallen wood, and thus escaped notice. After the war was over the affair was explained to Major Bradford by the Indian, and the marks of the wound in his side were shown."

Major Bradford held many positions of trust and responsibility in the colony. He was a deputy to the General Court from 1689 to 1691 He was the first representative to the General Court of Massachusetts from Plymouth He was the principal founder of the new town (Kingston) and a promoter of its interests by gifts of land for public purposes.

The General Court passed an Act in November 1717, setting off the north part of Plymouth, with a small portion of Plympton and Pembroke as a precinct or parish

By order of the General Court, Major Bradford issued on the 13th of August, 1720, the first warrant for a town meeting to be held on the 20th of the same month and at that meeting he was elected Moderator He deeded the land for the church and on June 15, 1721, he deeded a lot of land to the minister on which was soon erected the parsonage house

He married Feb. 6, 1674, Mercy Warren, daughter of Joseph Warren, with whom he lived 62 years Joseph was the son of Richard Warren, twelfth signer of the Mayflower Compact.

The ancestry of the Warren family has been traced by English writers to a Norman baron of Danish extraction The Normans and Danes were united in their efforts to make a settlement in the northern part of France, and ultimately succeeded in obtaining a footing in that part of the country of which from the former took the name of Normandy. One of these barons became connected by marriage with other distinguished families, among whom was a Danish Knight who "had Grennora, Herfastus, Wevia, Werina, Davelina and Sainfra.

"Of these, Grennora married Richard, Duke of Normandy, who had Richard, the father also of Richard, who, dying without issue, was succeeded in the dukedom by his brother Robert, the father of King William the Conqueror, who, by Maud, daughter of Baldwin, Earl of Flanders, had Robert Duke of Normandy, Richard, Duke of Bernav, in Normandy; William King of England, and several daughters, one of whom named Gundred, was married to William the first Earl of Warren and Surrey "

Richard Warren, the Plymouth Father, is of the same line of English ancestry as Peter Warren, the ancestor of Gen. Joseph Warren, who fell at Bunker Hill Richard Warren came in the Mayflower 1620, leaving wife, Elizabeth, and five daughters to come on the third ship 1623. He died in 1628. His children were.

MARY, who married 1628, *Robert Bartlett.*

Ann, married 19th April, 1633, Thomas Little
Sarah, married March 28th, 1634, John Cooke, Jr
Elizabeth, married 1636, Richard Church.
Abigail, married 1639, Anthony Snow, of Marshfield
Nathaniel and Joseph.

Joseph Warren, called in the Warren Genealogy, the oldest son of Richard, was held in high esteem   He was a representative by annual election 1681-6, and died in 1689.   He married Priscilla, daughter of John Faunce, and sister of the famous Ruling Elder, Thomas Faunce.

John Faunce, of Plymouth, came in the Ann, 1623, a young man   He married, 1633, Patience, daughter of George Morton, and had children, *Priscilla*, who married Joseph Warren; Mary, married July 13, 1658, William Harlow, Patience, married Nov. 29, 1661, John Holmes, Sarah, married Feb. 26, 1663, Edward Dotey; Thomas, born 1647; Elizabeth, 1648, Mercy, born 1657, married Nathaniel Holmes; John, Joseph.

Children of Major John Bradford.

Major John Bradford, by his wife, Mercy Warren, Bradford had issue:

I.   John, born Dec 25, 1675, married Rebecca Bartlett, of Duxbury.

II.   Alice, born June 28, 1677, married 1st, Edward Mitchell, Aug. 26, 1708, married 2d, John Hersey, of Hingham

III.   Abigail, born Dec. 10, 1679, married Gideon Sampson.

IV.   Mercy, born Dec. 20, 1681, married 1st, Jonathan Freeman, of Harwich, Mass.; 2d, Lieut. Isaac Cushman, Jr , of Plympton.

V.   Samuel, born Dec 23d, 1683, died March 26, 1710. He married Oct 21, 1714, Sarah Gray, daughter of Edward Gray of Trenton, son of Edward Gray, of Plymouth.

VI   Priscilla, born March 10, 1686, married Seth Chipman

VII   William (4), born April 15, 1688, married Hannah, daughter of Dea John Foster After his death she married George Partridge, of Duxbury, and had one son, Hon George Partridge.

THIRD GENERATION

Line of Major William Bradford, Eldest Son of Governor William Bradford by his Second Wife, Mrs Alice Southworth née Carpenter.

II WILLIAM BRADFORD. (3).   Second child of Major William and Alice (Richards) Bradford was born March 11, 1655.   He resided in Kingston, Mass., and died there in 1687

He married 1679, Rebecca Bartlett, of Duxbury, Mass , daughter of Benjamin, son of Robert Bartlett

This name was originally spelt Barttelot and the first of the family came to England with William the Conqueror, and seated himself at Ferring, county Sussex, and in the family pedigree is stated to have been buried at Stopham in 1100 where he had grants of

land   In the old Norman church at that place are marble slabs with inset figures of brass, showing a regular succession of Bartletts from John, deceased 1428, to the present time

The original coat armour of the Barttelot family was *Arms*—Sable, three sinister falconer's—gloves, argent, arranged triangularly, two above, one below, pendant, bands around the wrists and tassels golden

These were the arms for some centuries   Near the close of the 15th century, one of the crests, the castle, was granted to John Barttelot, who, in command of the Sussex troops, captured the castle of Fontenoy in France.

In the 16th century the swan crest was introduced to commemorate the right of the family to keep swans upon the river Arun, a right granted by William the Conqueror

Various quarterings have since been added through the allied families of the Bartletts The Gloucestershire branch, probably at a much later period were given *Arms*—Quarterly, per fesse indented argent and gules four crescents counterchanged.

Robert Bartlett, the Plymouth ancestor, was born at Gloucestershire, England, about 1606 and came to New England in 1623 in the *Ann*, the third ship which left the old country for Plymouth. He was the progenitor of W I Ashmead Bartlett, who married the Baroness Burdett Coutts.

Robert Bartlett was a prosperous farmer and settled in and around what was subsequently known as the Warren farm, near the "Pine Hills," in a district called Earl River, Plymouth, Mass, and he probably owned the whole domain of the second parish of Plymouth, called Manomet Ponds, and gave it to one of his sons. The old colony records contain his nuncupative will dated Sept. 19, 1696, and an inventory of his estate of the same date, which was also the year of his death. He married Mary, daughter of RICHARD Warren, of the Mayflower, twelfth signer of the Compact

Robert Bartlett by his wife Mary (Warren) Bartlett had issue Joseph and Benjamin.

Benjamin Bartlett, the second son of Robert and Mary (Warren) Bartlett, was born about 1633, died 1691. He was a man of some means for those days He had a farm valued at £140 and other property amounting to £250. He married Sarah Brewster (born about 1635), daughter of Love Brewster, who came with his father Elder William Brewster in the Mayflower.

Elder William Brewster, was born in England 1559-60. He was the son of William Brewster, who was appointed by Archbishop Sandys in January 1575-6, receiver of Scrooby and all its liberties in Nottinghamshire, and also baliff of the Manor House, to hold both offices for life

The Essex family of Brewsters, one of considerable antiquity bore *Arms*.—Azure a chevron ermine between three estoiles argent   Elder William Brewster was matriculated at Peterhouse College, Cambridge University, Dec 3, 1580. After leaving the University he entered into the service of William Davison, Queen Elizabeth's ambassador to Scotland and Holland, who found him so capable and faithful that he reposed the utmost confidence in him.   While negotiating with the United Provinces, Davison entrusted him with the keys of Flushing; and the States of Holland, in recognition of his merit, presented him with a golden chain. When, in 1587, Davison incurred the displeasure of the Queen, Brewster remained his steadfast friend

He held the office of Post of Scrooby from 1590 to 1607, succeeding his father. It was then an office under appointment from the government, and not, as afterwards, an employ-

Brewster.

ment for the accommodation of the public. While holding his official position, he occupied the Manor House at Scrooby, which had been the residence of archbishops and royalty. In Sept. 1607 he resigned his office.

Not agreeing with the forms of the Established Church he withdrew from its communion, and united with Rev. Richard Clifton and Rev. John Robinson. The newly formed Society met on the Sabbath at his house.

During the year 1608 he removed with the Nonconformist Society to Leyden, Holland and was appointed Elder of the Independent Church then fully organized. While residing in Leyden, he engaged there with Thomas Brewer, in publishing ecclesiastical treatises. This publication enraged King James I, through whose influence Brewer was imprisoned and Brewster's liberty was frequently imperilled. "He sailed in the Mayflower in 1620 and arriving at Plymouth, with the most submissive patience, bore the most trying hardships to which his old age was subjected, lived abstemiously, and after having been in his youth the companion of Ministers of State, the representative of his sovereign, familiar with the magnificence of courts, and the possessor of a fortune, sufficient not only for the comforts, but for the elegancies of life, this humble puritan labored steadily with his own hands in the field for daily subsistence. Yet he possessed that happy electricity of mind which could accommodate itself with cheerfulness to all circumstances; destitute of meat, of fish and bread, over his simple meal of clams, would he return thanks to the Lord, that he could "suck of the abundance of the seas, and of treasures hid in the sand." He enjoyed a healthy old age, and was sick but one day, when he died April 16, 1644. "The good Elder fought as he prays, and although he would far rather convert an enemy than hurt one, he would not dream of allowing him the first fire."

He left a library of over 300 volumes, (valued at £43) of which 64 were in the classic language. His whole estate was £150. He early removed to Duxbury, and settled in the neighborhood of Capt. Standish, and his house was afterwards occupied by his son Love. At his death his estate was divided among his two sons, who met after his funeral at Governor Bradford's in Plymouth, and in the presence of the Governor, Mr. Prence, Mr. Winslow and Capt. Standish, determined mutually on the division.

Many years ago, on a piece of land which was originally included in the limits of his farm was found a small silver spoon bearing the initials J. B.

A family tradition states that Elder Brewster planted on his farm the first apple tree in New England. At the time of the Revolution the original tree was gone; but there had sprung up from its roots another which was of a large size and known as the "Brewster tree."

His wife died in 1627. His children were:

I.   JONATHAN, born at Scrooby in Nottinghamshire, Aug. 12, 1598.

II   PATIENCE, born about 1600, came in the Ann, July 1623, died 1634, married Aug, 5 1624 Thomas Prince

III.   FEAR, born about 1603, came in the Ann 1623, died Dec. 12, 1684, married in 1627 to Isaac Allerton she being his second wife

IV   A child, died at Leyden June 20, 1609.

V.   LOVE came in the Mayflower 1620, married May 15, 1634, Sarah, daughter of William Collier of Duxbury, Mass

VI.   Wrestling, came in the Mayflower, 1620; Bradford says he "dyed a younge man unmarried" Subsequent research shows that Wrestling Brewster lived in Portsmouth, N H, married there and left children. The descendants maintain that he was the son of Elder William Brewster.

JONATHAN (1), settled in Duxbury, Mass, was one of the prominent men in the formation of its settlement, and in the establishment of its church. He sometimes practiced before the courts as an attorney, and is also styled gentleman He received grants of land in Duxbury, and likewise a ferry, (employing Peter Meacock in its management) He was frequently the town's deputy to the General Court. He removed to New London, Conn, and established by appointment a trading post on lands, purchased of Uncas, Chief of the Mohegans, and afterwards called Brewster's, Nick. He married Lucretia —— and had William, *Mary*, married John Turner, of Scituate, Nov 12, 1645, Jonathan, born 1627, Benjamin, who removed to Norwich, then to New London, where he married Anna Dart in 1659, and had Anna, 1662; Jonathan, 1664, Daniel, 1367, William, 1669, Benjamin, 1670

Love Brewster, fifth child and second son of Elder William Brewster, was admitted freeman 1636. He early removed to Duxbury and settled with his father by the bay side, and afterward sold the estate to Samuel Eaton. He married Sarah Collier, daughter of William Collier, one of the first settlers of Duxbury The will of Love Brewster is dated Oct 1, 1650 His children were:

I   SARAH, married about 1600, Benjamin Bartlett, son of Robert and Mary (Warren) Bartlett.

II.   Nathaniel, the eldest son, lived in Duxbury, Mass, and died in 1676. He married Sarah——but, as far as known, left no children

III   William

IV   Wrestling

Benjamin Bartlett (1) married for his 2d wife Cecelia —— 1678, who died about 1691 His children were all by the first wife.

Benjamin Bartlett (2) son of Benjamin (1) and Sarah (Brewster) Bartlett, inherited his father's farm and lands at Rochester and a double portion of his property He married Ruth, daughter of William Pabodie (or Peabody), son of John Pabodie William Pabodie of Duxbury, born 1620, died Dec 13, 1707, was a man much employed in public affairs, and of much respectability He married Elizabeth Alden, Dec. 26, 1644, daughter of John Alden, the Pilgrim, and Priscilla Mullens, his wife.

By his wife Ruth Pabodie Benjamin Bartlett (3) had·

1. Robert, born Dec. 6, 1679.
2. Benjamin.
3. MERCY, married to John Turner, of Scituate, Aug. 5, 1714.
4. PRICILLA, born January 1697, married to John Sampson, Dec 31, 1718.
5. DEBORAH, married to Josiah Thomas, Dec 19, 1723
6. RUTH, married to John Murdock, Jr
7. ABIGAIL born 1703, married to HON. GAMALIEL BRADFORD
8. REBECCA, born about 1705, married to JOHN BRADFORD, son of Major John, son of Major William Bradford
9. SARAH, born about 1707, married to Israel Bradford

CHILDREN OF WILLIAM BRADFORD (3), (PAGE 14) BY HIS WIFE REBECCA (BARTLETT) BRADFORD

I.   ALICE Bradford, born 1680, married William Barnes.
II   WILLIAM (4), born about 1682, died 1730, married Elizabeth Finney, daughter of Josiah Finney, son of 1st Robert, who married Elizabeth Warren
III   SARAH, born about 1684, married Jonathan Barnes   After his death she married Robert Stanford.

THIRD GENERATION

LIST OF MAJOR WILLIAM BRADFORD ELDEST SON OF GOVERNOR WILLIAM BRADFORD BY HIS
SECOND WIFE MRS. ALICE SOUTHWORTH NEE CARPENTER

III THOMAS BRADFORD. Third child of Major William and Alice (Richards) Bradford was born about 1660. By his father's will he received lands in Norwich, Conn , to which place he removed and died there 1703   In connection with his brother-in-law, Nehemiah Smith, Jr , he purchased land on the west side of Nehantic Bay, called the Soldier's Farm, having been given by the Legislature to five of Capt. Mason's soldiers for services in the Pequot war   On the north part of this land was a farm of 200 acres where Thomas Bradford settled. His home was not far from the northwest corner of what was then known as New London, but would now be in the town of Salem

In a recent work by Mary E Perkins, of Norwich, entitled " Old Houses Ancient Town of Norwich," etc , she says, on page 282   " As we now turn down the road leading to Dr. Gulliver's we come to the house which has always been regarded as the oldest of the Huntington homesteads. We have found from the records that this was the Bradford home lot, which, with the Bradford house, were sold to——Huntington, Jun'r, in 1691

" We are unable to say whether the present house was built in 1719, when the land was first given to Joshua [Huntington] or after 1710, by Jabez [Huntington]   In the latter case the house must have been the former house of Joshua, in the former the old Bradford homestead "

Thomas Bradford married Ann Smith, daughter of Nehemiah Smith, of Norwich, Conn

Nehemiah Smith was first of New Haven, 1645. He connected himself with the association that settled Norwich in 1660, and removed to that plantation, where he died in 1684. By his wife Ann, he had four daughters, Mary, wife of Samuel Raymond; *Ann*, wife of Thomas Bradford; Elizabeth, wife of John Raymond and Experience who was married 1st Nov. 1677 to Joshua Abel

CHILDREN OF THOMAS BRADFORD BY HIS WIFE ANN (SMITH) BRADFORD

I.   JOSHUA, born 1682, at Norwich, married 1712 Mary Brooks.

II.   JAMES, born 1684 at Norwich, married 1st Edith —— 2nd, Susanna.

III   Jerusha, baptized 1693 at Montville, died 1739, married 1716, Hezekiah Newcomb, of Lebanon, Conn., born about 1692, died 1772   He married 2nd, Hannah——

IV   WILLIAM, baptized at Montville, 1695

THIRD GENERATION

LINE OF MAJOR WILLIAM BRADFORD ELDEST SON OF GOVERNOR WILLIAM BRADFORD BY HIS SECOND WIFE MRS. ALICE SOUTHWORTH NEE CARPENTER

IV ALICE BRADFORD, fourth child of Major William and Alice (Richards) Bradford, was born about 1680, died 1745   She married 1st, March 29, 1679 Rev   William Adams of Dedham, Mass., son of William (2) son of William (1).

WILLIAM ADAMS was of Cambridge 1635 or earlier, admitted freeman 22 May 1639, removed to Ipswich probably before 1642. His children were *William*, Nathaniel, Samuel

WILLIAM ADAMS (2) son of William (1), born about 1620.   His children were John, *William*, born 27 May 1650.

REV. WILLIAM ADAMS (3) was born at Ipswich, May 27, 1650, died Nov. 17, 1685, graduated at Harvard 1671 and became pastor of the church at Dedham, Dec 3, 1673.   He was a successful preacher and was voted a salary of one hundred pounds   He married, 21 Oct. 1674, Mary daughter of William Manning, of Cambridge, and had Mary, born 12 Nov. 1675, died soon, Eliphalet, 26 March, 1677, a distinguished minister of New London, William, 17 Jan. 1679.   His wife died 24 June, 1679; he married, 29 March following, Alice, daughter of Major William Bradford.

CHILDREN OF ALICE BRADFORD BY HER MARRIAGE TO REV   WILLIAM ADAMS

1   ELIZABETH ADAMS, born Feb 23, 1681; married 1st Rev. Samuel Whiting of Windham, Sep. 4, 1696, when she was but sixteen years of age, and her children were distinguished, 1st Col. William Whiting engaged in the French war, 2nd. Rev   John Whiting of the second church in Windham (Scotland parish) and resigning his office he was judge of probate and also colonel; 3d, Col   Nathan Whiting, 4th, Mary, born 1712; married Nov   23, 1727, Rev   Thomas Clap, her father's successor in Windham and afterward President of Yale College, her daughter Mary Clap, who married Daniel Wooster of New Haven, and Temperance Clap, who married Timothy Pitkin, of Farmington

2.   ALICE ADAMS born April 3, 1682, married Rev. Nathaniel Collins, the first minister of Enfield, Conn   She died Feb 19, 1725, he died 1756

3   WILLIAM ADAMS, born Dec 17, 1683

4.   ABIEL ADAMS, was born Dec 15, 1685, after the death of her father, who died Aug 17, 1685.   She married 1707, Rev Joseph Metcalf, minister of Falmouth, a native of Dedham, born 1682, died May 24, 1720.   They had 11 children

After the death of Mr   Adams, Alice Bradford married in 1687, Major James Fitch, of Norwich, Conn., son of Rev. James Fitch, who was descended from a very distinguished English family of this name

Sir Thomas Fitch, the immediate progenitor of the American family of this name, was born in Bocking, England 1590, died 1645. He was a judge of much distinction and was created a baronet by Charles I. He married Anna Pew, who survived him and came to America with her three younger sons (two older ones emigrated previously). Some daughters and perhaps other sons, remained in England. The five sons who came to America were Thomas, Rev. James, Joseph, who settled at Windsor, Conn., and had three sons and two daughters, Samuel, who settled at Hartford and had two sons, and John who settled at Windsor and had no children.

The original spelling of the name was Ffytche, probably of Welch origin. The family from which Sir Thomas Fitch descended, resided at Thorpe Hall, county Lincoln, England, and was a branch of the family of Ffytche of Danbury Place and Woodham Walter, County Essex. This family bore *Arms*—Vert, a chevron between three leopards' heads or. *Crest*—A leopard's face or, pierced with a sword, in bend sinister ppr., hilt and panel of the first. *Motto*—Spes juvat

Rev. James Fitch, said to be son of Sir Thomas Fitch and Anna Pew, was born at Bocking, County of Essex England, Dec. 24, 1622. He was well advanced in his studies when he came to this country in 1638, at the age of sixteen. After a long and thorough course of preparation for the ministry under Revs. Hooker and Stone of Hartford, he was ordained in 1646 as pastor of the Congregational Church at Saybrook and remained there until 1660, when, with the greater portion of his congregation he removed to and founded the town of Norwich, and continued as pastor of the Norwich church until 1696, when he became disabled from further active service by a stroke of the palsy. In 1702 he retired to Lebanon, which he had previously founded and named, and where he spent the remaining years of his life. He was called by Cotton Mather "the holy and acute Mr Fitch." An election sermon, which he preached by invitation before the Colonial Assembly, received the compliment of being the first election sermon ever printed. To the Mohegan Indians he not only preached in their own language, but strove by gifts of his land to induce them to adopt the habits of civilization. This called forth a letter of thanks from the General Assembly of the Colony of Connecticut, accompanied by an appropriation for the use of his assistants, and a committal to his charge of the Indians captured in King Philip's War. To his influence, indeed, the colony was largely indebted for the co-operation of Uncas, Owaneco, and other Indians in that war, in which he had also served as a chaplain with such acceptableness as to call forth from the Assembly an urgent request that he would act again in the same capacity. He has been justly characterized as "a nice, kind and good man, and greatly beloved by his people, and who, during the fifty years of his ministry, exercised a beneficent and extended influence not only in spiritual matters but in secular affairs—in things pertaining to the welfare of the Colony and the good order and prosperity of the new plantations." Bishop Lee in a discourse delivered at the Norwich Jubilee some years since, said: ' He made early efforts to instruct the natives in the truths of the Gospel. He took pains to acquire their tongue and was a

frequent visitor in their wigwams. He impressed them with his own sincerity and benevolence, so that others, who, like Uncas himself remained obstinate in their unbelief, accorded him their entire confidence and regarded him with affectionate respect."

Rev. Mr. Fitch married 1st October, 1648, Abigail, daughter of Rev. Henry Whitfield, minister, of Guilford, Conn. She died Sep. 9, 1659. He married 20 October, 1664, Priscilla, daughter of Major John, and Anne (Peck) Mason. The children by his first wife (all born at Saybrook, Conn.) were *James*, born Aug. 2, 1649; Abigail, born August 1650, married Capt. John (son of Major John) Mason, Elizabeth, born January 1651, married Rev. Edward Taylor, of Westfield, Mass., Hannah, born Sep. 1653, Samuel, born April 1655; Dorothy, born 1658, became the second wife of Nathaniel Bissell, of Windsor, Conn. By his second wife Mr. Fitch had issue Daniel, born Aug. 16, 1670; Jabez, born April 1672, Ann, born April 1675, married Joseph (only son of Major William Bradford, of Plymouth, (by his second wife).

Major James Fitch, eldest child of Rev. James and Abigail (Whitfield) Fitch, was born Aug. 2, 1649. He was a prominent and influential man in his day, and the owner of a vast amount of land, which he accumulated by legislative grants, by purchase from other grantees, and through his intimate connection with the Indians, of whom he was a noted friend and patron. Indeed, after the death of Major John Mason, he possessed more influence over the sachems than any one else in the colony. In 1684 he received from Owaneco the native right and title to a large tract, extending from the Quinebaug River, north of the present town of Brooklyn, Conn., westward forty-five miles, and northward to beyond the northern boundary of Massachusetts. Out of this, in 1686, he sold the town of Pomfret, consisting of 15,100 acres, for £30. In 1687 he received from the same Chief parcels of land in Plainfield, and Canterbury, several miles in extent. In addition, also he owned land in various localities in the neighborhood of Norwich, and as one of Joshua's legatees, and an original proprietor of Windham, was allotted five one thousand acre shares, one located at Windham Centre, one at Willimantic, and three at Mansfield. He settled at Norwich, but lived in Preston, Plainfield and Canterbury, of which latter town he was the founder, having purchased the land, made the first clearing, laid it out in farm and house lots, and erected the first barn and framed house within its limits. He was a brave and experienced partisan soldier in the Indian wars, and active in politics, representing Norwich for several sessions, in the General Assembly, and was chosen in 1681, one of the Assistants of the Colony. An early patron of Yale College, to which he gave the glass and nails for its first edifice, he further renewed his interest by an endowment of 637 acres of land in Killingly township—an act which in the then peculiar situation of the infant institution (1701) insured its established permanence. He died in Canterbury, Conn., Nov. 10, 1727, aged 80.

Major Fitch married 1st, 1676, Elizabeth, youngest daughter of Major John Mason; she died Oct. 8, 1684. By her he had issue James, born 1678, died soon, James again born 1679, died early, unmarried, Jedediah born April 17, 1681, married Elizabeth, and had issue Elizabeth, Peter Samuel, born July 12, 1680, Elizabeth again, born 1684.

Major James Fitch married 2nd, Alice Bradford, daughter and fourth child of Major William Bradford.

CHILDREN OF ALICE BRADFORD BY HER MARRIAGE TO MAJOR JAMES FITCH, SON OF REV JAMES
FITCH.

1. ABIGAIL FITCH, born 1687; married 1703, Capt. John Dyer, of Canterbury, Conn

2. EBENEZER FITCH, born 1689-90, married 1712, Bridget Brown, possibly daughter of
Eleazer Brown, of Canterbury. She married 2nd, John Perry, of Ashford, Conn

3. DANIEL FITCH, born 1692; died 1752; married 1718, Anna Cook, possibly Stephen
Cook, of Canterbury, Conn

4. John Fitch, born 1695.

5. Bridget Fitch, born 1697.

6. JERUSHA FITCH, born 1699, died 1780; married 1717, Daniel Bissell, born 1694, died
1770. son of Daniel and Margaret (Dewey) Bissell of Windsor, Conn

7. William Fitch, born 1701.

8. COL JABEZ FITCH, born 1702, died 1784, married 1722, Lydia Gale, probably daughter of Richard Gale, of Canterbury, married 2d, Elizabeth Darby; married 3d, —— King

9. LUCY FITCH, born about 1700, married 1719, Henry Cleveland, born about 1697, son
of Josiah and Mary Cleveland, of Canterbury

10 THEOPHILUS FITCH, born about 1703; died 1751 "awfully" He married Mary Huntington, born 1707.

11. Alice Fitch.

THIRD GENERATION

LINE OF MAJOR WILLIAM BRADFORD, ELDEST SON OF GOVERNOR WILLIAM BRADFORD BY
HIS SECOND WIFE MRS ALICE SOUTHWORTH NEE CARPENTER

V MERCY BRADFORD, fifth child of Major William and Alice (Richards) Bradford, was
born in 1660. She was married Sep 16, 1680, to Samuel Steel, of Hartford, Conn , son of
John Jr., son of John Steel, the ancestor

John Steel was born in county Essex, England; came to New England with his wife and
children and was living in Dorchester, Mass., 1630, a proprietor of New Town, now Cambridge, Mass , 1632, admitted freeman 1634. He removed to Hartford, Conn , was representative to the General Court and Secretary 1636-37, magistrate, and one of the founders
of Hartford 1635, one of eight representative men appointed to govern Connecticut 1636,
Secretary of the colony four years, and one of the founders of Farmington, Conn , where
he died in 1665. He married 1st, Rachel——probably in England, she died in 1653, he
married 2d, Nov 23, 1656, Mercy, widow of Richard Seymour. He had six children of
whom John was the eldest.

JOHN STEEL (2), son of John (1) and Rachel (——) Steel, was born probably in England, died in 1653 He married 1645, Mercy, daughter of Andrew Warner, of Hartford.
They had Benoni, Henry, Daniel, Mary, Lieut. John, Samuel.

Samuel Steel, youngest son of John Steel, was born March 15, 1652, married Sep 16,
1680, Mercy, daughter of Major William Bradford He died 1710, she died 1720.

CHILDREN OF MERCY BRADFORD BY HER MARRIAGE TO SAMUEL STEEL

1.   THOMAS STEEL, born Sep 9, 1681; married May 10, 1700, Susanna Webster Steel

He died 1757, she died Nov. 27, 1757   They resided at West Hartford, Conn

II.   SAMUEL STEEL, born Feb. 15, 1684, died 1710, unmarried.

III   JERUSHA STEEL, twin of Samuel, married——Smith, lived in Hartford

IV.   William Steel, born Feb. 20, 1687, died 1713; unmarried

V.   ABIEL STEEL, born Oct. 8, 1693; married Dec 5, 1712, John Webster   He died 1753, at Southington, Conn

VI.   DANIEL STEEL, born April 3, 1697, married 1725, Mary Hopkins.   He died May 28, 1770, at West Hartford

VII   ELIPHALET STEEL, born Jan 23, 1700; married Catharine Marshfield   He died July, 1773; she died June 7, 1788, at West Hartford.

THIRD GENERATION.

LINE OF MAJOR WILLIAM BRADFORD, ELDEST SON OF GOVERNOR WILLIAM BRADFORD BY

His SECOND WIFE MRS. ALICE SOUTHWORTH NEE CARPENTER

VI HANNAH BRADFORD, sixth child of Major William and Alice (Richards) Bradford was born May 9, 1662; died May 28, 1758. She married Nov. 28, 1682, Joshua Ripley, of Hingham, Mass , and removed with him to Windham County, Conn   She was evidently a woman of superior education for the Windham records state that she was " a noble and useful woman, and remarkable, not only for intelligence and accomplishments, but for her skill in the art of healing "   She was the first and for a long time the only physician in the settlement, and it is said that the first male physician, Dr. Richard Huntington, received much of his medical knowledge from her.

Joshua Ripley, her husband, was the son of John, son of William Ripley, the ancestor.

William Ripley, with his wife, two sons and two daughters, came from Hingham, Norfolk County, England, on the ship Diligent, with his wife and family, and settled in Hingham, Mass , in 1638   His second wife, whom he married Jan 28, 1657-8, in this country, was the widow of Thomas Thaxter, of Hingham, England and Hingham, Mass. William Ripley died July 20, 1656, leaving *John*, Abraham and Sarah

JOHN RIPLEY, son of William Ripley, was born in England; came with his parents to America; died at Hingham, Mass , Feb. 2, 1683. He married Elizabeth, daughter of Rev. Peter Hobart, first pastor of the church at Hingham, who died in 1692 in the 60th year of his age.   They had seven children of whom *Joshua* was the third

Joshua Ripley, son of John and Elizabeth (Hobart) Ripley, was born in Hingham, Mass., May 9, 1658, died May 18, 1739. He moved from Hingham to Norwich, Conn., in 1689, and later to Windham County, Conn , where he bought of Isaac Magowan, the first settler, sixty acres of land on both sides of Merrick s Brook. The first town meeting in Windham was held June 11, 1692, when Joshua Ripley was appointed town clerk, he was also town treasurer. He was a man widely known and respected as of sterling sense and judgment. He was one of the first justices of the peace in Connecticut, and was appointed May 1698, when that office was first instituted   He was also one of the seven pillars or counsellors and justices of the quorum in 1726.

CHILDREN OF JOSHUA AND HANNAH (BRADFORD) RIPLEY

I.   ALICE, born in Hingham, Mass., Sep. 18, 1683, married Samuel Edgerton, of Norwich, Conn

II.   HANNAH, born in Hingham Mass., March 2, 1685, married Samuel Webb, of Windham, Conn., Oct. 8, 1711.

III. FAITH, born in Hingham, Sep 20, 1686; married Samuel Bingham, of Scotland, Conn

IV.   JOSHUA born in Hingham, May 13, 1688; married Mary Backus, of Windham, Dec. 3, 1712 He died Nov 18, 1773

V.   MARGARET, born in Norwich, Conn., Nov. 4, 1690, married ——Seabury, of Lebanon, Conn

VI LEAH, born in Windham, Conn., April 17, 1693, married 1st, amuel Cook, 2d, James Bradford, of Canterbury, Conn

VII RACHEL, twin sister of Leah, born in Windham, April 17, 1693, married Winslow Tracy, of Norwich, Conn

VIII HEZEKIAH, born in Windham, Jan 10, 1695, married Miriam Fitch, Oct 16, 1740; married 2d, Mary Skinner, of Windham, Nov 25, 1746. He died Feb 7, 1779.

IX.   DAVID, born in Windham, May 20, 1697. married Lydia Carey, of Windham, March 21, 1720, died Feb 16, 1781

X.   IRENE, born in Windham, Aug. 28, 1700; married Samuel Manv, April 20, 1719

XI.   JERUSHA, born in Windham, Nov. 1, 1701, married Edward, of Windham, Sep. 9, 1724

XII. ANN, twin sister of Jerusha, born in Windham. Nov 1, 1701; married Dr. Solomon Wheat, of Windham.

THIRD GENERATION.

LINE OF MAJOR WILLIAM BRADFORD ELDEST SON OF GOVERNOR WILLIAM BRADFORD BY HIS SECOND WIFE MRS ALICE SOUTHWORTH NEE CARPENTER

VII IRELATIAH BRADFORD. seventh child of Major William and Alice (Richards) Bradford, was born about 1664, was married to John Steel, of Norwich, Conn, son of James, son of George (2), son of George (1)

GEORGE STEEL (1) presumed to have been an elder brother of John, who married Mercy Bradford, 5th child of Major William Bradford, came to New England with him   He was admitted a freeman at Cambridge, Mass., in 1654, removed thence to Hartford, Conn., was a proprietor of land there in 1639, died 1663, "very old." He had four children of whom *James* was the youngest

JAMES STEEL, youngest child of George Steel, was born probably in England   He married 1st, Anna Bishop, supposed to have been a daughter of John Bishop, of Guilford, she died 1676, he married 2d, Bethia, widow of Deacon Samuel Stocking, (by whom she had eight children)   The Colonial records show that James Steel, in 1657-8, was enlisted as a trooper in the war against the Pequots   In 1662 he was appointed by the General Court,

with William Wadsworth, to lay out lands in Hammonasset [Killingworth] He was appointed 1672 with others to run the dividing line between the towns of Lyme and New London for which service he was allowed by the Court six pounds and fifteen shillings out of the public treasury The Court granted him the same year 160 acres of land for a farm. In 1675 he was appointed commissary in King Philip's war and was allowed at the rate of fifty pounds per annum as compensation for his services. His dwelling house was on the old plan of Hartford, south of Little River He had issue Sarah, Lieut. James, *John*, Mary, Elizabeth, Rachel

John Steel, son of James and Anna (Bishop) Steel, born about 1660, married Melatiah daughter of Major William Bradford; after his death she married————Stevens, of Killingworth. Her sister May married Samuel Steel

CHILDREN OF JOHN AND MELATIAH (BRADFORD) STEEL.

I.   BETHIA born about 1688-9, married May 17, 1709, Samuel Shepard, born Feb. 2, 1684, died June 5, 1750 (she died 1746). He was the son of John Shepard, of Hartford who married May 12, 1680, Hannah daughter of Deacon Paul Peck, son of John Shepard, of Cambridge, Mass., 1750, and Hartford, Conn, 1766, who married 1649, Rebecca daughter of Samuel Greenhill, son of Edward Shepard of Cambridge, Mass, 1637.

II.   JOHN, born 1693; died unmarried

III.   EBENEZER, born 1695, married Susanna————of West Hartford He removed to Killingworth and purchased lands there Feb. 23, 1723 He died 1746.

THIRD GENERATION

LINE OF MAJOR WILLIAM BRADFORD ELDEST SON OF GOVERNOR WILLIAM BRADFORD BY HIS SECOND WIFE, MRS. ALICE SOUTHWORTH NEE CARPENTER.

VIII CAPC. SAMUEL BRADFORD, eighth child of Major William and Alice (Richards) Bradford, was born in 1668, died Feb. 17 1714. He resided at Duxbury where his name appears on the records as early as 1700. He had a grant of land adjoining his house lot.

His gravestone in Duxbury Cemetery contains the following inscription· "Here lyes Capt Samuel Bradford of Duxbury, who died Feb. 17, 1714 in ye 47th year of his age." He was called Capt. Samuel Bradford He was a juryman 1700, constable 1701, selectman 1702 and in 1710 was one of three men appointed to divide the Common Lands.

He married Hannah Rogers, daughter of John and Elizabeth Rogers, of Duxbury, Mass., son of John the ancestor.

John Rogers, who was of Plymouth 1631, bought land in Duxbury of Edward Chandler. He was a representative to the General Court in 1657 In his will of Feb 1661, he calls himself of Marshfield and names wife and six children, besides grandchildren, George and John Russell His wife was named Frances. They had *John* (2), Joseph, Timothy (freed from bearing arms, being lame) Ann, married John Hudson, Mary, Abigail.

John Rogers (2) son of John (1) and Frances Rogers, died in 1696. He married Elizabeth Peabody Nov. 1666, daughter of William Peabody, of Duxbury, born 1619, married Dec. 26, 1644, Elizabeth, eldest daughter of John Alden the Pilgrim John Rogers (2) by his

wife Elizabeth (Peabody) Rogers had issue *Hannah*, born Nov. 16, 1668, married Samuel Bradford, son of Major William Bradford

　　　　CHILDREN OF SAMUEL BRADFORD (VIII) AND HANNAH (ROGERS) BRADFORD

I. HANNAH, born Feb. 14, 1689, married Nathaniel Gilbert, of Taunton, Mass

II. GERSHOM, born Dec. 21, 1691, married Priscilla daughter of Rev. Ichabod Wiswall, of Duxbury He removed with a part of his family to Bristol R. I. In 1714, having previously resided in Kingston, Mass. They had issue

1. ALEXANDER, born about 1718, who died leaving one son Alexander? and one daughter.

2. DANIEL, born 1720, married 1st, Mary Church, 2d, Susan Jarvis, died 22 July 1810 He settled in Bristol and became the ancestor of a numerous posterity His oldest child, Priscilla, born 12th March 1752, married 15th Jan. 1775, Col. Sylvester Child, of Warren, R I, born 1752, died Jan 9, 1832 There were by this marriage three daughters Mary R , who married Christopher Child; Priscilla Bradford, who married Shubael P Child, and Abigail Miller, who married John Fessenden and had John M. of Jamaica Plains and Guy M. of Warren, R. I

3. NOAH, married Hannah Clark.

4. JOB, married Elizabeth Parkman He was born in Kingston and settled in Boston.

III PERCY BRADFORD, born Dec. 28, 1694 He resided in Attleboro, Mass , where he died Jan. 19, 1746. He was a graduate of Harvard and a member of the Council of Massachusetts He married Abigail Belch

IV. ELIZABETH, born Dec 15, 1696, married William Whiting of Hartford, Conn

V. JERUSHA, born March 10, 1699, married Rev. Ebenezer Gay, of Hingham

VI WELTHIA, born May 15, 1702 She married Peter Lane, of Hingham, Mass , born 25 May, 1697, son of Ebenezer, son of George, son of William Lane, of Dorchester, Mass

VII. HON. (AND COL.) GAMALIEL born May 18, 1704, died in Duxbury, Mass., April 24, 1778 He was a member of the Council of Massachusetts and Judge of the County Court He was known as the "Hon. Gamaliel Bradford" He shared largely in all the duties of public offices of the town and was always selected to bear the responsibilities of its important agencies He was a friend of education, and did much toward the maintenance and improvement of the public schools He represented the town in the Legislature from 1761 to 1770, and was a member of the executive council. He was for many years a justice of the peace and judge of the county court. He also had command of a company of militia in his native town, and about 1750, was raised to the rank of Major and later Colonel of the regiment. He married Abigail Bartlett, of Duxbury, Mass , daughter of Benjamin Bartlett and Sarah Brewster, son of Robert Bartlett, who married Mary, daughter of Richard Warren, a Mayflower Pilgrim.

　　　　　　　THIRD GENERATION

LINE OF MAJOR WILLIAM BRADFORD, ELDEST SON OF GOVERNOR WILLIAM BRADFORD BY HIS SECOND WIFE, MRS ALICE SOUTHWORTH NÉE CARPENTER

IX **MARY BRADFORD**, ninth child of Major William and Alice (Richards) Bradford, was

born about 1669 She was married to William Hunt, son of Ephraim, son of Enoch.

The Massachusetts State Archives, lib 129, folio 16, contains the following in reference to the Hunt family, of Weymouth, in a deposition of James Humphrey

"Enoch Hunt, of Titenden in the Parish of Lee about two miles distant from Wendon, and Ephraim Hunt the reputed eldest son, removed into New England and for some time dwelt in Weymouth The said Enoch Hunt, the father, soon returned back to England, but his son Ephraim remained, and settled at Weymouth, and there married a wife, by whom he had several sons, and continued his dwelling there unto the time of his decease"

EPHRAIM HUNT, of Rehoboth 1644 son of Enoch, was born in England, removed thence to Weymouth; married 1st Sarah Baker. He married 2nd, Ebbet, and had issue Thomas, Ephraim, John. William, 1655, Enoch, 1657, and Joseph. He was admitted freeman 1671, was captain of the train band   His will is dated April 7, 1687.

WILLIAM HUNT, son of Ephraim, was born about 1655. He is called of Chilmark He lived at Martha's Vineyard After the death of his first wife, he married Sarah, widow of Samuel Bradford, brother of Mary, his first wife

THE CHILDREN OF WILLIAM HUNT, BY HIS WIFE MARY BRADFORD (HUNT), WERE
1 Mary Hunt, born Feb 8 or 18, 1687.
2. William Hunt, born May 17, 1693

THIRD GENERATION

LINE OF MAJOR WILLIAM BRADFORD ELDEST SON OF GOVERNOR WILLIAM BRADFORD BY HIS SECOND WIFE MRS. ALICE SOUTHWORTH NEE CARPENTER

X SARAH BRADFORD, tenth child of Major William and Alice (Richards) Bradford, was born about 1671 She was married to Kenelm Baker, of Marshfield, Mass , son of Samuel, son of Rev. Nicholas Baker, the ancestor

Rev. Nicholas Baker was one of the first settlers of Hingham Mass , and from this circumstance it is supposed he came from Hingham, in Norfolk, England He received a share in the first division of house lots in Hingham in 1635 He afterward became an extensive landholder in Hull, and resided there. He was engaged in agricultural pursuits for several years, though a man of more than ordinary qualifications, and often employed in public affairs He was a deputy to the Mass Colony Court (the May session) in 1636, it being the sixth Court that had been holden, but the first in which Hingham was represented Again he was a deputy to the May Court in 1638 After the death of President Dunster he was invited to preach at Scituate First Church He was ordained in Scituate in 1660 He died in 1678 By wife Grace he had *Samuel*, Elizabeth, Nicholas, Deborah, Sarah, Mary.

SAMUEL BAKER, of Duxbury, son of Rev Nicholas Baker, was born about 1630 He married Eleanor Winslow, daughter of Kenelm Winslow, brother of Gov Edward Winslow. By her he had *Kenelm*, born 1657; Lydia 1659, Elizabeth 1661, Mary 1662, Alice 1663, Ellen 1665 His second wife, whom he married in 1677, Patience was Simmon, by whom he had a son *Samuel*

KENELM BAKER, eldest son of Samuel and Eleanor (Winslow) Baker, was born in Duxbury, Mass., in 1657. He married Sarah Bradford 10th child of Major William Bradford

CHILDREN OF KENELM BAKER AND SARAH BRADFORD

I. KENELM BAKER, married Patience Doten, of Marlborough, at Duxbury, Jan. 22, 1719
II. SAMUEL BAKER, married Miss Ford, of Marshfield, Mass.

THIRD GENERATION

LINE OF MAJOR WILLIAM BRADFORD (THROUGH HIS SECOND WIFE WIDOW WISWALL) ELDEST SON OF MAJOR WILLIAM BRADFORD BY HIS SECOND WIFE MRS. ALICE SOUTHWORTH NEE CARPENTER.

XI LIEUT. JOSEPH BRADFORD, only child of Major William Bradford by his wife, Widow Wiswall Bradford, was born in 1675. He lived in Lebanon, Conn., of which he was an original proprietor, also at New London, Conn.

A Court of Commission was held at his house on the Mohegan lands, Feb. 22, 1721 to "hear, review and settle all disputes respecting the Indian lands." He frequently occupied public positions, which he filled with honor and credit. He represented the town of Lebanon in the State Legislature in 1707-8-9-12 and 1714. In 1702 he was commissioned Ensign of the train band, of which he became Lieutenent before 1710, Selectman 1710, 1714

He married Anne Fitch (born April 1675 died 1715) daughter of Rev. James Fitch of Norwich, Conn., Oct. 5, 1678. [See Fitch family page 20]

CHILDREN OF LIEUT. JOSEPH BRADFORD AND ANNE FITCH, DAUGHTER OF REV. JAMES FITCH

1. Ann, born July 26, 1699
2. Joseph } twins born April 9, 1702.
3. Priscilla }
4. Sarah, born Sep. 21, 1706
5. Hannah, born May 24, 1709.
6. Elizabeth, born Oct. 21, 1712.
7. Althea } twins again, born Sep. 19, 1715.
8. Irene }
9. John, born May 20, 1717

Anne, wife of Joseph, died Oct. 7, 1717. He moved to Mohegan that year and is said to have married 2nd Mary (Sherwood) Fitch, widow of Daniel Fitch.

THIRD GENERATION

LINE OF MAJOR WILLIAM BRADFORD ELDEST SON OF GOVERNOR WILLIAM BRADFORD BY HIS SECOND WIFE MRS. ALICE SOUTHWORTH NEE CARPENTER.

XII ISRAEL BRADFORD, twelfth child of Major William Bradford and eldest child by his wife Mary Atwood (Holmes) Bradford; was born in Kingston, Mass., about 1679 and resided there. He married in 1701, Sarah Bartlett, of Duxbury, Mass., daughter of Benjamin and Ruth (Peabody) Bartlett, son of Benjamin (1) son of Robert the ancestor, who married Mary Warren, daughter of Richard Warren of the Mayflower.

CHILDREN OF ISRAEL BRADFORD BY HIS WIFE SARAH BARTLETT.

I.   Ruth, born Dec. 11, 1703, died Feb. 1713

II   Bathsheba, born Feb 1703, married Thomas Adams

III.   Benjamin, born Oct. 17, 1705, married 1st Zeresh Stetson 2nd Mary Chitman   Resided in Kingston

IV.   Abner, born Dec 25, 1707; married Susanne Porter, resided in Kingston.

V.   Joshua, born June 23, 1710, married Hannah daughter of Elisha Bradford and removed from Kingston to Madiencock (now Freedom) Me, where on May 27, 1756 he and his wife were killed by a party of Indians, who, at the same time, carried their children to Canada, where they remained in captivity until Quebec was taken by Gen Wolf, when they returned to Madiencock

VI.   Ichabod, born Sep. 22, 1713; married Mary Johnson, Nov 25, 1743.   She died July 1761.

VII. Elisha, born March 26, 1718, no issue

THIRD GENERATION

LINE OF MAJOR WILLIAM BRADFORD ELDEST SON OF GOVERNOR WILLIAM BRADFORD BY HIS SECOND WIFE MRS ALICE SOUTHWORTH NEE CARPENTER.

XIII EPHRAIM BRADORD, thirteenth child of Major William, and second child by wife Mary Atwood (Holmes) Bradford, was born about 1685.   He resided in Kingston, Mass. He married Feb. 13, 1710 Elizabeth Bartlett   She may have been a daughter of Samuel Bartlett of Northampton, Mass, who had a daughter, Elizabeth, born 1687.   He was a son of Robert Bartlett, the Hartford, Conn. settler.   The contemporary name of Elizabeth does not appear among the descendants of Robert Bartlett, of Plymouth.

CHILDREN OF EPHRAIM BRADFORD BY HIS WIFE ELIZABETH BARTLETT.

I   Deborah, born June 21, 1712, died Jan. 10, 1732.

II.   Anna, born July 25, 1715

III.-   Elizabeth, born Nov. 3, 1717.

IV.   Ephraim, born Jan 1, 1719

V.   Abigail, born Feb 28, 1720.

VI   Susanna, born May 5, 1721.

VII. Elijah, born Jan. 23, 1723

VIII   Ezekiel

IX.   Simeon, born Aug. 28, 1729.

X   Wait.   *Hait*

THIRD GENERATION

LINE OF MAJOR WILLIAM BRADFORD ELDEST SON OF GOVERNOR WILLIAM BRADFORD BY HIS SECOND WIFE MRS. ALICE SOUTHWORTH NEE CARPENTER

XIV-3 DAVID BRADFORD, fourteenth child of Major William Bradford and third child of Mary (Atwood Holmes) Bradford, was born in Kingston, Mass, about 1690, died there March 16, 1730.

He married in 1714, Elizabeth Finney (or Phinney), born about April 11, 1690, daughter of John Finney, son of John (2), son of John (1)

John Finney, of Plymouth, by wife Christian, who died 9th Sept. 1649 had *John*, born 24th Dec., 1638 and perhaps others. He removed to Barnstable, and married June 10, 1650, Abigail, widow of Henry Coggen, who died May 6, 1653. He married 3d, Elizabeth Bayley, and had eight children.

John FINNEY (2), son of John (1), was born Dec. 24, 1638, married Aug 10, 1664, Mary Rogers, and had twelve children, of whom John (3) was the eldest.

John FINNEY (3), son of John (2), was born May 5, 1665, married May 30, 1689, Sarah Lombard, daughter of Thomas, son of Bernard, son of Thomas

Thomas Lombard, of Dorchester, Mass., came in the "Mary and John" 1630, bringing Bernard and two other children. He was admitted freeman Oct 9, 1630. He removed later to Scituate and thence to Barnstable

Bernard Lombard, son of Thomas, came with his father to Mass in 1630. He went to Scituate April 1, 1634, and, with his wife, joined the church April 19, 1635. He went thence to Barnstable with Lathrop. He had Thomas and other children.

Thomas Lombard, son of Bernard, born about 1640, married Dec 23, 1665, Elizabeth Darby or Derby and had Sarah

Sarah Lombard, daughter of Thomas Lombard, was born Dec 1666, married John Finney (3).

John FINNEY (3), by wife Sarah (Lombard) Finney, had *Elizabeth*, who was married to David Bradford

CHILDREN OF DAVID BRADFORD BY HIS WIFE ELIZABETH FINNEY

I.   NATHANIEL, born Dec. 10, 1715, married Sarah Spooner, of Plymouth, granddaughter, probably, of William Spooner, who was of Plymouth 1637 and of Dartmouth 1660, and Hannah, daughter of Joshua Pratt

II   Jonathan, born Nov. 13, 1717; no issue

III LYDIA, born Dec 23, 1719, married 1st, Elkanah Cushman 1740, 2d, Lazarus Le Baron, 1743. She, Lydia, died 1757

IV   NATHAN, born April 3, 1722, married 1st, Elizabeth ———— she died April 30, 1773; married 2nd, Sarah Sturtevant, 1776 He had no issue by second wife. He died Oct 14, 1787.

THIRD GENERATION

LINE OF MAJOR WILLIAM BRADFORD ELDEST SON OF GOVERNOR WILLIAM BRADFORD BY HIS SECOND WIFE MRS SOUTHWORTH NEE CARPENTER

XV HEZEKIAH BRADFORD, fifteenth child of Major William Bradford, was born probably in Kingston, about 1692, where he continued to reside

He married Mary Chandler, of Duxbury, Mass., born 1704, daughter probably of Joseph son of Joseph, son of Edmond

Edmund Chandler, of Roxbury 1635, owned land near R Hicks, which he sold to John Rogers, and also land to Isaac Robinson In 1636 he had granted to him forty acres of

land lying on the east side of Meyses Symonson, where Morris formerly began to clear for the Bowmans " He was of Scituate 1650   He died 1662, (will dated May 3, 1662), leaving an estate of £38   He owned land at Barbadoes which he gave to his daughters Sarah Anna and Mary. He had another daughter Ruth and sons Benjamin, Samuel and *Joseph.*

JOSEPH CHANDLER (1), son of Edmund, was of Sandwich 1661, and of Duxbury 1681.   He had John, *Joseph* and perhaps Edmund, of Duxbury 1710 and Benjamin 1681, who died March 25, 1771, aged 87.

JOSEPH CHANDLER (2), son of Joseph (1), was born about 1675, married Feb 12, 1701, Martha Hunt, and had Philip 1702; *Mary,* born Aug. 3, 1704, Joshua, Zechariah 1708; Edmond, 1710, Ebenezer, 1712, Sarah, 1711, Martha, 1716, Jonathan, 1718; Judah, 1720)

MARY CHANDLER, second child of Joseph (2), was born Aug 3, 1704, married, probably to Hezekiah Bradford

Hezekiah Bradford, by his wife Mary (Chandler) Bradford, had a daughter Mary

SECOND GENERATION

LINE OF JOSEPH BRADFORD YOUNGEST CHILD OF GOVERNOR WILLIAM BRADFORD, BY HIS SECOND WIFE MRS. ALICE SOUTHWORTH (NEE CARPENTER.)

[see 9th page]

JOSEPH BRADFORD, fourth and youngest child of Governor William and Alice (Southworth nee Carpenter) Bradford was born in 1630, died July 29, 1715   He resided in Kingston (then Plymouth) on Jones River, half a mile from the mouth at a place called Flat House Dock, perhaps from the circumstances that he lived in a house with a *flat roof*

He married May 25. 1664 Joel (born 1643) daughter of Rev. Peter Hobart, son of Edmund.

Edmund Hobart, the progenitor of the family in America was born in Hingham, Norfolk England emigrated to New England in 1633, and settled in Hingham Mass. where he died in 1646 He represented the town of Hingham at the General Court of Mass from 1639 to 1642.

Rev. Peter Hobart, son of Edmund was born in Hingham England in 1604   He attended the free school at Lynn and entered the University at Cambridge, and after teaching a grammar school, held a a pastorate in Haverhill, Suffolk until 1635   In the summer of that year he came with his wife and four children to New England   and with his father who had preceded him—together with a few others formed a new plantation which they called Hingham, where he organized the First Church (Congregational), of which he continued as pastor until his death   Four of his sons, graduates of Harvard were Congregational clergymen, one of whom was the successor of John Eliot, in 1764.

His children who came with him were. Joshua, Jeremiah, Josiah, Elizabeth, who married John Ripley

Those born here were. Ichabod 1635, died soon, Hannah, 1637, died soon, Hannah again, born 1638, married John Brown, of Salem, Bathsheba, born 1640, married Joseph Turner of

Scituate, Israel, born 1642.

Jael, born Dec 1643, married May 23, 1664, Joseph Bradford.

Gershom, 1645, Japhet, April 1647, Nehemiah, 1649, David, 1651, Rebecca, born 1654 married Oct 10, 1679, Daniel Mason, of Stonington, Conn , Abigail Lydia   Rev Peter Hobart, died Jan. 20, 1679

CHILDREN OF JOSEPH BRADFORD BY HIS WIFE JAEL HOBART BRADFORD.

I   Joseph, born April 18, 1665.

II.   ELISHA, married 1st Hannah Cole and had Hannah, who married Joshua Bradford of Kingston   He married 2nd Bathsheba La Broche.

LINE OF JOSEPH BRADFORD YOUNGEST CHILD OF GOVERNOR WILLIAM BRADFORD BY HIS SECOND WIFE MRS ALICE SOUTHWORTH NEE CARPENTER.

II Elisha Bradford, son of Joseph and Jael (Hobart) Bradford, was a native of Plymouth in New England   The "Female Review" says of him   "He possessed good abilities and explored many sources that led him to literary distinction   As he was eminent in property; so piety, humanity and uprightness were the distinguishing characteristics of his life."   He was married Sep 7, 1719, to Bathsheba Le Broche, a French lady of elegant extraction and accomplishments.   Her father was a native of Paris   Mr Bradford, for one of his benevolent offices, being bound for a ship and rich cargo, belonging to a merchant of the same town, had the misfortune to lose the greater part of his interest.   Being at this time (1760) considerably advanced in years, this circumstance, together with the loss of his eldest son, preyed fast upon his constitution, and he did not long survive to mourn the loss of what seemed not in his power to remedy "

　　CHILDREN OF ELISHA BRADFORD BY HIS WIFE BATHSHEBA LE BROCHE.

1.   Hannah, born April 10, 1719.

2.   Joseph, born Dec. 17, 1721

3.   Nehemiah, born July 27, 1724

4.   Laurana, born March 26, 1720, married Elijah McFarland, of Plympton.

5.   Mary, born Aug. 1, 1727.

6.   Elisha, born Oct 6, 1729.

7.   Lois, born Jan. 30, 1731

8   DEBORAH, born Nov 18, 1732, married Jonathan Sampson, Jr.

This Deborah Bradford, eighth child of Elisha and Bathsheba (Le Broche) Bradford by her marriage to Jonathan Sampson, Jr , became the mother of one of the most remarkable women of the Revolution   Jonathan Sampson, Jr , her husband, was the son of Jonathan Sampson and Joanna Lucas, son of Isaac Sampson born 1660, married Lydia Standish, daughter of Alexander, son of Capt. Miles Standish, he was the son of Abraham Sampson, the ancestor

Jonathan Sampson, by his wife Deborah (Bradford) Sampson, had a child *Deborah*, who, served in the ranks of the patriot army throughout the War of the Revolution in male attire, without her sex having been discovered.

Grinnell and Allied Families.

THE ancestry of the Grinnell family among the early settlers of America presents a remarkable combination of men who were well known in their day

The Mayflower ancestry, beginning with the line of Governor Bradford, includes five signers of the Mayflower compact, together with their own and allied families, who were among the "Blessed Company", six colonial governors, also deputy governors, magistrates, assistants, judges, lawyers, clergymen, military leaders, etc

Matthew Grinnell, the ancestor, is first found at Newport, R I , where he was admitted freeman in 1638 He was probably one of the numerous Huguenot refugees who fled from France to Holland after the Revocation of the Edict of Nantes.

Of the children named in the will of Matthew are Matthew, Thomas and *Daniel* His wife's name was Rose, her surname does not appear in the records

Daniel Grinnell, son of Matthew and Rose Grinnell, was born in 1636 He married Mary Wodell, born 1640, daughter of William and Mary Wodell They lived at Portsmouth and Little Compton, R I. They had issue, *Daniel* (2), Richard and Jonathan.

Daniel Grinnell (2), son of Daniel (1), and Mary Wodell Grinnell, was born at Little Compton about 1665 He married Lydia Pabodie, daughter of William Pabodie, son of William Pabodie, the ancestor

WILLIAM PABODIE, the ancestor, was born in England, 1619, and was an early settler of the Plymouth Colony The Plymouth records state that he was "a man much employed in public affairs, and of much respectability " While not himself a Pilgrim he had the honor of marrying the daughter of a Pilgrim, Elizabeth Alden, born 1622 or 3, the *first white woman born in New England* They were married Dec 26, 1644 He with others, purchased in 1659, from the Seaconet tribe of Indians a large tract of land known by the name of Seaconet Point now Little Compton, R I Until 1745 this was a part of Massachusetts William Pabodie was one of the "twenty-nine persons who appeared at Plymouth, July 22, 1673 and proved their respective shares on the grant of land at Seaconet " He moved with his family to their new home in 1684

John Alden, the Pilgrim, the father of Elizabeth (Alden) Pabodie, was the seventh and youngest signer of the Mayflower Compact He was born in 1599, and had only just realized his majority when he put his name to the important document His "powers of persuasion" were evidently appreciated by his friend Captain Miles Standish, and it was no fault of his that while acting as "proxy" in the courtship of the beautiful Priscilla Mullens or Molines he became the principal, and she thus became the mother of the first white child born in Plymouth Colony. Her father was William Molines, or as appears among the signers, William Mullins

WILLIAM MOLINES, tenth signer of the Mayflower Compact, formed a part of the little colony at Leyden, Holland, where the Pilgrims met and formed their plans for the new settlement He was one of the Huguenot refugees, and was descended probably from the ancient family of De Moulins He died Feb 21, 1621, "pious and well deserving, endowed also with considerable outward estate, and had it been the will of God that he had survived might have proved a valuable instrument in his place " His will refers to his wife Alice and two children, who were left in England, a son William and a daughter Sarah

WILLIAM PABODIE, who married Elizabeth Alden, daughter of John Alden and Priscilla Molines, had a daughter Lydia (born April 3, 1667, died July 15, 1748,) who married Daniel Grinnell (2)

Daniel Grinnell (2), by his wife Lydia (Pabodie) Grinnell, had Priscilla born 1689, Pabodie born 1691, and *George*, born about 1700 These were probably all born at Saybrook, Conn , where the father had removed some time previous

PABODIE GRINNELL eldest son of Daniel and Lydia (Pabodie) Grinnell, born in 1691 married Ruth Nettleton

George Grinnell, (1) youngest child of Daniel (2) and Lydia (Pabodie) Grinnell, was born about 1700 in Saybrook, Conn He married Mary Bull, daughter of Edward, son of John Bull,

JOHN BULL was born at Dennington in the parish of Stowe, County of Gloucester, England, about 1637 His wife Hannah, as appears by the Saybrook records, was born at the same place February 3, 1639 John Bull settled first in Hartford, Conn , and removed thence to Saybrook He was probably engaged in the Pequot war, as his name appears in the list of those referred to in the following

"Feb 7, 1678 The Town agreed that the Souldiers that went out of the Town in the Indian war shall have five acres apiece of Land, etc " John Bull, by his wife Hannah, had Edward and others

EDWARD BULL, son of John and Hannah Bull, was born in the parish of Stowe, County of Gloucestershire, England, September 12, 1662, came with his parents to New England and settled in Saybrook He married Mary Post and had several children, of whom *Mary* was one She was married to George Grinnell

George Grinnell, by his wife Mary (Bull) Grinnell had seven children, of whom William was the eldest

William Grinnell, son of George and Mary (Bull) Grinnell, was born 1726 He married Mary

William Grinnell died in 1761 as appears by the following, from the Colonial Records of Connecticut

"Upon the memorial of Daniel Grinnell, administrator of the estate of William Grinnell late of Saybrook, deceased, representing to this Assembly that the debts and charges due from said estate surmount the personal estate of said deceased £79 6s , 9d lawful money, and pray-

ing for liberty to sell so much of the real estate of said deceased as shall be sufficient to raise said sum with the incident charges arising thereon, Resolved, by this Assembly, that Joseph Spencer of Saybrook have liberty to sell so much of the real estate of said deceased as shall be sufficient to raise the said sum with the incident charges arising thereon, taking the directions of the Court of Probate in the district of Guilford therein."

William Grinnell by his wife Mary (——) Grinnell, had a son George

George Grinnell, (2) son of William and Mary Grinnell, was born in Saybrook, Conn., July 14, 1750, died at Greenfield, Mass., March 1, 1844. He married Lydia Stevens, daughter of Col. Jonathan Stevens, son of Capt. James Stevens, of Amherst, Mass.

CAPT. JAMES STEVENS, born November 31, 1686, lived in Amherst, Mass., married 1713 Dorothy Frye, of Amherst, Mass.

They had, among other children, *Jonathan*   **1605475**

COL. JONATHAN STEVENS, son of Capt. James and Dorothy (Frye) Stevens, was born at Andover, Mass., 1727. He served with distinction in the War of the Revolution. His first service was as private in Capt. Johnson's company, Col. Johnson's regiment of Massachusetts militia. In the Historical Sketches of Andover, page 377, appears the following.

"PAWLET, Oct. 1st, 1777

"*Loving Sister* — This will inform you that I am very well at present, and have been so ever since I came from home, and I hope you and all my friends enjoy the same state of health

"We have been up to Ticonderoga and took almost four hundred prisoners of the British army and returned one hundred of our men that were prisoners there

"Our army have come from Ticonderoga down as far as Pawlet, about sixty miles, and expect to march to Stillwater very soon. So no more at present. I remain

Your loving brother,

JONATHAN STEVENS

"To the Widow Lidia Peters in Andover."

COL. Jonathan Stevens married Lydia Felch, daughter of Ebenezer Felch and Lydia Chandler

(EBENEZER FELCH runs back to the Gov. Bradford line. An Ebenezer Felch born 1689, married Bridget Brown.)

Col. Jonathan Stevens, by his wife Lydia Chandler, had issue Lydia, who married George Grinnell (1)

GEORGE GRINNELL, by his wife Lydia (Stevens) Grinnell, had *George* (8)

Hon. George Grinnell, (3) son of George and Lydia (Stevens) Grinnell, was born in Greenfield, Franklin Co., Mass., December 25, 1786, graduated at Dartmouth College in 1805, studied law and was admitted to the bar in 1811. One of his first speeches to attract public attention appears to have been made in the year 1818, when he was only thirty years of age, at the convention which decided upon the location of Amherst Academy, which afterwards became Amherst College. Of this convention the History of Amherst College says

"After which George Grinnell, Esq., who was secretary of the Convention, left his seat, taking his place in the aisle, and also delivered a very powerful and effective speech, still keeping the full attention of the Convention. The speech produced a new and different feeling throughout the house; and the result, when the vote was taken, was in favor of Amherst as the location of the College. The argument of Mr. Grinnell, delegate from the 'Poll Parish' in Greenfield was particularly convincing and is said not only to have carried the suffrages of the Convention but to have brought him so favorably before the public as to have had not a little influence in preparing the way for his election to Congress."

He was Prosecuting Attorney for Franklin County from 1824 to 1827, and was a representative in Congress from Massachusetts 1829 to 1839 and during this period was associated with all the great statesmen of the age, among whom were Clay, Webster, Calhoun, Adams, Polk, as well as many of the lesser lights. He took a leading part in all the great questions of the day, and his name appears quite as often in the columns of the Congressional Record as that of any man in Congress. He introduced and carried through many important measures. Probably no man in Congress did as much for improving the condition of the army, and in promoting the interests of the Revolutionary veterans and their widows and orphans as did he. Many a veteran or widow of a veteran would have become an inmate of the poorhouse or have been left to starve but for his efforts in calling the attention of Congress to their condition and introducing measures for their relief. He urged upon Congress the increase of pay of army officers, which up to that time remained the same as during the Revolution. He introduced a resolution "to inquire into the expediency of extending the benefits of five years' half pay now allowed by law to the widows and orphans of officers and soldiers of the militia and volunteers who died in the service of the United States, to the widows and orphans of officers and soldiers of the regular army who have died or shall die in the service, or in consequence of wounds received in the line of duty."

Mr. Grinnell took strong grounds in favor of the abolition of slavery in the District of Columbia, and though not a pronounced Abolitionist, in the general sense was one of the pioneers in the movement which had its inception in that early day.

In December, 1838, he introduced a resolution in the petition presented from certain inhabitants of Nantucket, praying Congress to open international relations with the Republic of Hayti. His most active opponent was Henry A. Wise, of Virginia. The Congressional Report states that

"Mr. Grinnell, who was entitled to the floor, addressed the House at some length in support of the petition—a right, he insisted, which had never been denied by the veriest despot on earth. He then expatiated on the great advantages that would accrue to this country by opening commercial negotiations with, and acknowledging the independence of Hayti, where we now labored under great disadvantages, owing to the inequality of duties between goods carried in American vessels and in those of other nations which had recognized the nationality of that Republic. Mr. Grinnell admitted that it did look to one sort of abolition, and that alone, viz.: the abolition of national distinctions founded on color, to which he was at a loss to conceive any possible objections."

On returning from Congress Mr Grinnell gave his attention to the public affairs of his own State, and, though never an office seeker, he held public office up to the day of his death. From 1838 to 1859 he was a member of the Board of Trustees of Amherst College, and in 1854 the degree of LL D was conferred upon him by that institution. He was for four years—1849 to 1853—Probate Judge of Franklin County. He was President of the Troy and Greenfield R R and was prominent in other business enterprises. In politics he was identified with the old Whig party, and as Presidential Elector in 1840 he voted for William Henry Harrison. He was foremost in all works of benevolence and public improvement in his native town.

Mr Grinnell married Eliza Seymour Perkins, daughter of Rev Nathan Perkins, son of Nathan, son of Matthew, son of Deacon Joseph, son of Jacob, son of Joseph, son of John Perkins the ancestor.

The family of Perkins were originally settled in Warwickshire, and became possessed of the manors of Orton on the Hill, Morebarne Beanhills, and the Westons by purchase in the reign of Charles II. They bore *Arms*, Sable, an eagle, displayed, ppr, on a canton dexter argent, a fesse, dancette of the first, quartering Steele Farmer, Beardsley, Shirley, Duncomb, kirkpatrick, Sharpe. *Crest*, a unicorn s head, issuing out of a ducal coronet. Motto *Toujours loyale*

JOHN PERKINS, the ancestor, was born at Newent, England in 1590, died at Ipswich, Mass, 1654. He sailed in the ship Lyon for New England in 1630, arrived at Boston 1631, removed thence to Ipswich in 1633, admitted freeman, 1631, representation to the General Court 1636, He married, about 1613, Judith --——, and had issue *Jacob* and other children

JACOB PERKINS, son of John and Judith Perkins, was born in England, 1624, came to New England with his parents at the age of seven. He died at Ipswich, Mass, Jan 29 1700. He was a farmer and Sergeant of the train band. He married, first, in 1647, Elizabeth Lovell, daughter of Thomas Lovell. He married, second, Mrs Demaris Robinson, widow of Nathaniel Robinson, of Boston. By his first wife he had *Joseph* and others

DEACON JOSEPH PERKINS, tenth child of Jacob and Elizabeth (Lovell) Perkins, was born at Ipswich, Mass, June 24, 1674, died at Norwich, Conn, Sept 6, 1726. He married Martha, daughter of Joseph and Dorothy (Parke) Morgan, (born 1680, died Sept 6, 1726) The inventory of his estate was £2757, and included three farms viz the homestead of 310 acres, and two others comprising nearly 1000 acres. By his wife, Dorothy (Morgan) Perkins, he had *Matthew* and other children

MATTHEW PERKINS, son of Joseph and Dorothy (Morgan) Perkins, was born at Norwich, Conn, Aug 31, 1713, died at Lisbon, Conn, May 3, 1773. He was a prosperous farmer and owned 1000 acres of land. He married Hannah Bishop. They had twelve children, among whom was Rev Nathan Perkins, D D

REV NATHAN PERKINS, D D, son of Matthew and Hannah (Bishop) Perkins, was born May 12, 1749 and died June 18, 1835. He was for sixty five years pastor of the church at West Hartford. He married Catharine Pitkin, born Feb 22, 1757, daughter of Rev Timothy Pitkin, of Farmington, Conn son of Governor William (3), son of William (2), son of William Pitkin the ancestor

HON. WILLIAM PITKIN, the progenitor of the family in America, who came from England in 1659, was possessed of great ability and tenacity of purpose. He was admitted freeman Oct. 9, 1662, and was appointed the same year Prosecutor for the Colony, and was appointed, by the King, Attorney General in 1664. From 1675 to 1690, a period of fifteen years, he annually represented Hartford in the Colonial Assembly. In 1676 he was chosen Treasurer of the Colony. He was often appointed by the Colony of Connecticut Commissioner to the United Colonies. In 1676 he and Major Talcott were appointed to negotiate peace with the Narragansett and other Indians. In 1690 he was elected a member of the Colonial Council, and continued to hold this position until his death. He was one of the principal planters of the Colony, having purchased a large tract of land on the east side of the river.

He married Hannah, daughter of Hon. Ozias and Mary (Woodward) Goodwin, the progenitor of the Goodwin family in Connecticut. The latter was born in England, 1596, and came to New England in company with Rev. Thomas Hooker and others. His wife was the daughter of Robert Woodward, of Braintree, County Essex, England. William Pitkin, by his wife Hannah (Goodwin) Pitkin, had eight children, of whom William (2) was the second.

HON. WILLIAM PITKIN (2), son of William (1) and Hannah (Goodwin) Pitkin, was born 1664 died April 5, 1723. He was educated by his father in the profession of the law. He was Judge of the County and Probate Courts, and Court of the Assistants from 1702 till 1711. Upon the establishment of the Superior Court, in 1711, he was appointed Judge of that Court, and in 1713 he was made Chief Justice of the Supreme Court. He represented Hartford in the General Assembly in 1696. In 1697 he was elected one of the Council of the Colony and was annually re-elected for twenty-six years till his death. He was one of the commissioners to receive the Earl of Belmont on his arrival in New York. He was Commissioner of War 1706-7. He was one of the committee to prepare the manuscript laws of the Colony in 1709, also committee on the revision of the laws. In 1718 he was appointed one of a committee of three by the General Assembly to build the first State House in the Colony at Hartford. He was a military officer in the company of his brother Roger. He built in 1706 two fulling mills at Pitkin Falls, and did a large business in clothing and woolens in addition to his professional labors. He married, Oct. 24, 1689, Elizabeth, daughter of Capt. Caleb Stanley, and sister of his brother Roger Pitkin's wife. They had eleven children, of whom *William* (3) was the fourth child and eldest son.

GOVERNOR WILLIAM PITKIN (3), son of Hon. William (2) and Elizabeth (Stanley) Pitkin, was born April 30, 1694, died Oct. 1, 1769. He was distinguished both in public and private life. He acquired from his father a thorough knowledge of business and public affairs, particularly of the laws and policy of the Colony. This, with his natural courtesy and ease of manner, soon brought him prominently before the public. He represented Hartford in the Colonial Assembly from 1728 to 1734. He was appointed Captain of the "train band" in 1730, and rose to the rank of Colonel in 1739. He was elected Speaker of the House in 1732, and was elected to the Council in 1734. He was Judge of the County Court from 1735 to 1752. He was appointed Judge of the Superior Court in 1741. He was Chief Justice of the Superior Court twelve years,

and Lieutenant Governor from 1754 to 1766, about twelve years   He was a strong advocate of colonial rights, and the first in the Colony to resist the "Stamp Act," which was passed in 1765, when Fitch was Governor and Pitkin Lieutenant Governor   When Governor Fitch and others of his Council, who thought it their duty, were taking the oath to support the "Stamp Act," Lieut Gov Trumbull and others of the Council remonstrated and left the Council Chambers while the oath was taken by Governor Fitch and his supporters   At the next election May, 1766 when both Fitch and Pitkin were candidates for Governor, Pitkin was elected by a majority "so great" says the *Connecticut Gazette* of the day, "that the votes were not counted "   The great popularity of Governor Pitkin and his policy in resisting the "Stamp Act," and his sudden removal by death while in office, gave to his deputy, Trumbull, the Governorship at the following election

At the first meeting of the Colonies to form a plan of union, in 1754, Lieut Gov Pitkin and five others, with Benjamin Franklin as chairman were chosen a committee by the Colonies, to meet at Albany, N Y, and prepare a Constitution   The plan then presented was the germ of the Articles of Confederation, rearranged by Franklin in 1775, and adopted in 1777, under which the Colonies lived till the adoption of the Federal Constitution

Governor Pitkin married Mary Woodbridge, daughter of Rev Timothy and Mabel (Wyllys) Woodbridge, the sixth minister of the First Church of Hartford, son of Rev John (2). son of Rev John Woodbridge (1)

REV. JOHN WOODBRIDGE, of England, died Dec 9, 1637, was rector of the parish of Stanton, near Highworth in Wiltshire, and a man "so able and faithful," says Cotton Mather, "as to obtain a high esteem among those that at all know the invaluable worth of such a minister " He married Sarah Parker, daughter of Rev Robert Parker, a learned English divine "who did so *virtuously* that her own personal character would have made her highly esteemed if a relation to such a father had not farther added unto the lustre of her character "   They had issue John (2)

REV JOHN WOODBRIDGE (2), son of Rev John (1) and Sarah (Parker) Woodbridge, was born 1613, died July 1, 1691   He became a Nonconformist, and at the age of twenty-one came to New England in the ship "Mary and John," in company with his uncle, Rev Thomas Parker, and settled in Newbury, Mass   In 1643 he taught school in Boston   He, with others, negotiated the purchase from the Indians of the plantations on which the town of Andover grew up He was ordained at Andover, Oct 24, 1645, this being one of the earliest, if not the earliest, of the regular ordinations in New England   He returned in 1647 to England with his wife and family, was Chaplain of the Parliamentary Commissioners who treated with the King at the Isle of Wight, and afterwards minister at Andover, Hants and Barford, St Martin (Wiltshire), until he was ejected at the Restoration   He returned to New England in 1663 and was made assistant to his uncle Rev Thomas Parker, at Newbury, remaining in office till Nov 3, 1670 He was assistant of the Massachusetts Colony, 1683-4, and died at Newbury, March 17, 1695 He married Mercy Dudley (born Sept 27, 1621, died July 1, 1691), daughter of Governor Thomas Dudley of the Massachusetts Colony

GOVERNOR THOMAS DUDLEY, third Governor of Massachusetts Bay, was born in Northamptonshire, England, in 1576, died at Roxbury, Mass., July 31, 1653. He was the son of Capt. Roger Dudley. He obtained leave from Queen Elizabeth to volunteer his services under Henry IV, of France, says a tradition, at the siege of Amiens, and afterward helped to retrieve the fortune of the Earl of Lincoln by the faithful stewardship of his estates. A principal member of the Massachusetts Company which settled in Boston and vicinity, he came over in 1630 with the commission of Deputy Governor, which office he held till 1640, and again from 1645 till 1650. In 1644 he was appointed Major General of the Colony. After residing in Cambridge, Ipswich and Boston, he finally settled in Roxbury, where his estate was long possessed by his descendants. By his wife Dorothy —— he had *Mercy* and other children.

MERCY DUDLEY, daughter of Governor Thomas and Dorothy (———) Dudley, was baptized in England Sept. 27, 1621. She was married to Rev. John Woodbridge.

REV. JOHN WOODBRIDGE, by his wife Mercy (Dudley) Woodbridge, had issue *Timothy* and others.

REV. TIMOTHY WOODBRIDGE, son of Rev. John and Mercy (Dudley) Woodbridge, was born at Barford, St. Martins (Wilts), came (on his father's return) to New England in 1663, graduated at Harvard College in 1675, became a member of the First Church in Hartford, Conn., in 1683 but was not ordained till Nov. 1685. He was one of the principal ministers of the Connecticut Colony named as trustees and authorized by the General Assembly of Connecticut to found Yale College in 1699, was a Fellow of Yale from 1700 to 1732, and was offered the Rectorship after the resignation of Rector Cutler in 1722, was a prominent member of the Saybrook Convention in 1708. He married *Mehitable*, daughter of Samuel Wyllys, widow of Rev. Isaac Foster, and also of Rev. Daniel Russell, of Charlestown, Mass.

SAMUEL WYLLYS, the father of Mehitable Woodbridge, was the son of Governor George Wyllys.

GOVERNOR GEORGE WYLLYS, born at Fenny Compton, County Warwick, was the son of Richard Wyllys and Hester, daughter of George Chambers of Williamscote, County Oxford, Eng. His pedigree is traced back in England for several generations. In Camden's Visitation of Warwickshire in 1619 George Wyllys is described as living at Fenny Compton, with his wife Bridget, daughter of William Young, of Kingston Hall. The name of the wife he brought with him to New England was Mary ——, probably a second wife. In 1636 he sent his steward, William Gibbons, with twenty men, to Hartford to purchase and prepare for him a farm and dwelling house, and have everything in readiness for himself and family. He had been a partner with Robert Salstonstall and William Whiting in the Dover and Piscataqua patents. His homestead included the site of the famous Charter Oak. He married in Hartford in 1638, was chosen magistrate April 11, 1639, again in 1640, '43 and '44, Deputy Governor 1641, Governor 1642, and was one of the Commissioners of the United Colonies. He died in Hartford, March 9, 1644. His fourth child was *Samuel*.

SAMUEL WYLLYS, son of Governor George Wyllys, was born in 1632 in England, came with his parents to New England and was graduated at Harvard College, 1653. He was chosen

magistrate in 1654, and continued in that office until 1685 In the absence of the Governor and Deputy Governor he was repeatedly appointed Moderator of the General Court In 1661-2, 1664 and 1667 he was one of the Connecticut Commissioners for the United Colonies He was extensively engaged in trade and often absent from the Colony conducting his business affairs with the West Indies He was Assistant, 1680 to 1683 He married Ruth, daughter of Governor John Haynes

GOVERNOR JOHN HAYNES, born 1594, was the son of John Haynes, of Old Holt, who purchased the manor and estate of Copford Hall He came to New England in the "Griffin," arriving Sept 3, 1633 with Rev Thomas Hooker He was admitted a freeman of Massachusetts May 14, 1634, chosen Assistant and Governor next year, again Assistant in 1636 He removed in May, 1637, to Hartford Conn , of which he was an original proprietor He presided over the deliberations of the General Court November, 1637, and continued to do so until he was chosen the first Governor of Connecticut, April 11, 1639 He was elected Governor alternate years until his death, and chosen Deputy Governor 1640, '41 '46, '50 '52, interchanging with Edward Hopkins He married, Dec 27, 1614 Mabel Harlakenden daughter of Richard Harlakenden, of Earle's Colne Priory, County Essex , she was baptized at Earle's Colne, Dec 27, 1614 Her pedigree extends in an unbroken line to William the Conqueror. By his wife, Mabel Harlakenden, Governor Haynes had a daughter, *Ruth*, who was married to Samuel Wyllys

SAMUEL WYLLYS (son of Governor George Wyllys) had, by his wife Ruth (Haynes) Wyllys, a daughter *Mehitable*, who was married to Rev Timothy Woodbridge

REV TIMOTHY WOODBRIDGE, by his wife, Mehitable (Wyllys) Woodbridge (widow of Rev Isaac Foster, also of Rev Daniel Russell) had issue, *Mary*, who married Governor William Pitkin

GOVERNOR WILLIAM PITKIN by his wife Mary (Woodbridge) Pitkin, had issue five children, of whom *Rev Timothy Pitkin* was the second

REV TIMOTHY PITKIN, son of Gov William and Mary Woodbridge Pitkin, was born June 13, 1727 , died July 18, 1812 He was graduated at Yale in 1747 , tutor there 1750 to 1751 , from 1777 to 1804 was a Fellow of the Yale College Corporation , was one of the beneficiaries of Yale to the amount of one hundred and fifty pounds (£150) He studied theology and was installed pastor of the Congregational Church at Farmington, Conn He was one of the trustees of Yale College for many years, and when Dartmouth (N H) College was instituted he was chosen one of the Board of Trustees for it

He married Temperance Clap, daughter of Rev Thomas and Mary (Whiting) Clap, son of Stephen, son of Samuel, son of Thomas, son of Richard Clap, of England

DEACON THOMAS CLAP, son of Richard was born in Dorchester, Eng ; in 1597 came to New England with his brothers John and Richard He was at Dorchester, Weymouth, and in 1640 settled at Scituate He was admitted freeman in 1636 , deacon of the church at Scituate and a representative of the General Court He married Abigal —— and had issue, *Samuel*

MAJOR SAMUEL CLAP, son of Deacon Thomas and Abigal Clap, was born about 1641   He succeeded to his father's residence   He was Major of militia and a man of some importance in town   He married Hannah, daughter of Thomas Gill, who married Hannah, daughter of the first John Otis   They had ten children of whom *Stephen* was the third

LIEUT (and Deacon) STEPHEN CLAP, son of Major Samuel and Hannah (Gill) Clap, was born at Scituate Mass, in 1670   He was deacon of the church, Ensign and Lieutenant of the "train band"   He married Temperance Gorham, daughter of John Gorham son of Capt John Gorham

CAPT JOHN GORHAM, son of Ralph, was born in England, baptized at Benefield, Northamptonshire, June 28, 1621   His father Ralph and grandfather James, resided at Benefield Northhamptonshire   His descent is traced from De Goran of La Jannere near Gorran in Maine, on the borders of Brittany   He came with his father Ralph to Plymouth in 1637   He commanded a company in the sanguinary battle at the "Swamp Fort" in the Narraganset country, Dec 19, 1675, and died from exposure and fatigue at the age of 54   He married Desire, eldest daughter of *John Howland* the Pilgrim in 1643

John Howland, the Pilgrim, thirteenth signer of the Mayflower Compact, was born in Essex County England, in 1592   Bradford in his journal makes the following reference to him on the Mayflower voyage   "In a mighty storm John Howland, a passenger, a stout young man, by a keel of ye ship, was thrown into the sea   But pleased God, he caught hold of ye Topsail Halliards we hung overboard, and ran out ye length, yet he kept his hold the several fathoms under water, till he was drawn up by ye rope to ye surface, and by a boat hook and other means got into ye ship ; and tho' some't ill upon it liv'd many years, and became a useful member both in church and Commonwealth "   He "took to wife" Elizabeth, daughter of John Tilley

John Tilley, sixteenth signer of the Mayflower Compact, was born in England about 1582   He married Elizabeth (Carver) for his first wife, and by her had a daughter *Elizabeth*

ELIZABETH TILLEY, daughter of John Tilley and Elizabeth (Carver) Tilley, was born 1607, died Dec 20, 1687, married Aug 14 1623, John Howland

JOHN HOWLAND by his wife Elizabeth (Tilley) Howland, had, among other children, a daughter *Desire*, (named from Desire Minter, who was a kind friend of her mother's orphaned girlhood), married Capt John Gorham in 1643

CAPT JOHN GORHAM, by his wife Desire (Howland) Gorham, had ten children, of whom John (2) was the third

LIEUT COL JOHN GORHAM, son of John (1) and Desire (Howland) Gorham, was born in Marshfield, Mass, Feb 20, 1651   He served under his father in King Philip's war   On June 5, 1690, he was appointed a Captain in the unfortunate Canada expedition, and subsequently Lieut Colonel of the militia   He was a man of sound judgment and good business capacity   He died Dec 9, 1716   He married, Feb 16, 1694, Mary, daughter of John Otis, and sister of

the famous Colonel John Otis   They had nine children, of whom *Temperance* was the second

TEMPERANCE GORHAM, daughter of Lieut. Colonel John and Mary (Otis) Gorham, was born Aug. 2, 1678, married Stephen Clap

STEPHEN CLAP, by his wife Temperance (Gorham) Clap had a son Thomas

REV THOMAS CLAP, son of Stephen and Temperance (Gorham) Clap, was born in 1703, died in 1765; graduated at Harvard College in 1722, and was one of the most distinguished men of his time   He was ordained at Windham, Conn, 1726, chosen President of Yale College 1740 and continued in the chair until 1764, when he resigned   President Stiles says of him " He studied the higher branches of mathematics and was one of the first philosophers America has produced, and equaled by no man except the most learned Professor Winthrop "   As President he was most indefatigable and successful in promoting the interests of learning and raising the rank of his college   He married Mary Whiting, daughter of Rev. Samuel, son of Rev John, son of William Whiting the ancestor

HON WM WHITING, the American ancestor of the Connecticut branch of the Whiting family, came to New England in 1633, and resided for three years in Newtown (now Cambridge), removing thence with Rev Thomas Hooker and others to Hartford, Conn, of which he was an original proprietor   Frequent mention is made of him as "one of the fathers of the colony "   He was referred to in the town records as "William Whiting, Gentleman "   He was several times representative to the General Court, was one of the Magistrates in 1642, was chosen Treasurer of the Colony in 1641, and continued in that office till his death   By his wife Susanna, he had issue, *John*

REV JOHN WHITING, son of Hon   William and Susanna (———) Whiting, was born in 1625, graduated at Harvard College in 1653 ; preached several years at Salem, Mass , was ordained over the First Church in Hartford, Conn , 1660   He married Sybil Collins, daughter of Deacon Edward Collins of Cambridge, and had a son, *Samuel*

REV SAMUEL WHITING, son of Rev   John and Sybil (Collins) Whiting, was born at Hartford, Conn , in 1670 , died at Enfield, Conn , in 1725   He married Elizabeth Adams, daughter of Rev William Adams, of Dedham, Mass

REV WILLIAM ADAMS, (son of William (2) son of William Adams (1) of Cambridge, in 1635, or earlier, was born at Ipswich, Mass , May 27, 1650, died Nov 17, 1685 ; married 1st, Mary, daughter of William Manning, married 2nd, *Alice*, daughter of Major William Bradford, son of Governor William Bradford   (See page 19)

They had issue, Elizabeth Adams, born Feb 23, 1680, who was married Sept 4, 1696, to Rev. Samuel Whiting

REV SAMUEL WHITING, by his wife Elizabeth (Adams) Whiting, had several children, among whom was *Mary*

MARY WHITING, daughter of Rev Samuel Whiting was born in 1712, married Nov. 23, 1724, Rev Thomas Clap

REV THOMAS CLAP, by his wife Mary (Whiting) Clap had issue, Temperance and Anne

TEMPERANCE CLAP, eldest child of Rev Thomas and Mary (Whiting) Clap, was born April 29, 1732, she married Rev Timothy Pitkin

REV TIMOTHY PITKIN, by his wife Temperance (Clap) Pitkin had eight children, the second of whom was *Catharine*

CATHARINE PITKIN, second child and eldest daughter of Rev Timothy and Temperance (Clap) Pitkin, was born Feb 22, 1757, married Rev Nathan Perkins

REV NATHAN PERKINS D D, by his wife Catharine (Pitkin) Perkins, had a son, Nathan

REV NATHAN PERKINS (2), son of Rev Nathan and Catharine (Pitkin) Perkins, was born at West Hartford, Conn, Aug 26, 1776. He was graduated at Yale and preached for a number of years at Amherst

He married Mabel Seymour, daughter of Col Timothy Seymour, son of Capt Timothy, son of Timothy, son of John, son of John son of Richard

RICHARD SEYMOUR the ancestor was one of the original settlers of Hartford in 1636. He removed to Norwalk in 1651, where he died in 1655. By his wife Mercy ——— he had a son, John, died 1713, married Mary Watson and had John (2)

JOHN SEYMOUR, son of John and Mary (Watson) Seymour, was born at Hartford, Conn, June 12, 1666, died there May 7, 1748. He married, Dec 19, 1693, Elizabeth Webster, daughter of Robert, son of Governor John Webster

GOVERNOR JOHN WEBSTER was one of the original settlers of Hartford in 1636, and was said to have come from County Warwick, England. He was a representative to the General Court, May, 1637, Magistrate 1639 to 1655, when he was made Deputy Governor and next year Governor. In the great contest about church government he took sides with Rev Mr Russell, of Wethersfield, which resulted in his removal, with others, in 1659, to found the town of Hadley, Mass. He was admitted freeman of Massachusetts in May, 1660, made Magistrate there, and died there April 5, 1661. He married and had a son, Robert

ROBERT WEBSTER, son of Governor John and ——— Webster, was born about 1620, died 1676. He resided in Hartford and removed thence to Middletown. He married Susanna, daughter of Richard Treat

RICHARD TREAT was born in England probably London, about 1590, died in Wethersfield Conn, 1669. He was a leading man in the Colony and held many public offices, and was one of the nineteen to whom the charter of Connecticut was granted April 23, 1662. He married, first, Joanna ———, second, Alice Gaylord, who survived him. He had, among other children, Governor Robert and *Susanna*, who married Robert Webster

ROBERT WEBSTER, by his wife Susanna (Treat) Webster, had *Elizabeth* who married John Seymour

JOHN SEYMOUR, by his wife Elizabeth Webster, had Timothy

TIMOTHY SEYMOUR son of John and Elizabeth (Webster) Seymour, was born at Hartford, Conn, June 27, 1696, died at West Hartford, Sept 8, 1749. He married, April 27, 1727, Rachel

Allen (born Aug 20, 1694), daughter of Edward and Rachel (Steele) Allen, of Boston They had Timothy

CAPTAIN TIMOTHY SEYMOUR, son of Timothy and Rachel (Allen) Seymour, was born Feb 21, 1728, died 1784, married Dec 1, 1718, Lydia Kellogg (born July 22, 1729, died Nov 6, 1810)

COL. TIMOTHY SEYMOUR, son of Capt Timothy and Lydia (Kellogg) Seymour, was born in West Hartford about 1750 He married Abigal Skinner, daughter of Timothy, son of John (3), son of John (2), son of John (1)

JOHN SKINNER of Hartford, was one of Rev Thomas Hooker's party and was an original proprietor It is supposed he came from Braintree, County Essex England He married Mary daughter of Joseph Loomis, Sen , and had John

JOHN SKINNER (2), son of John (1) and Mary (Loomis) Skinner, was born in 1641, died Oct 27, 1743 He married Mary, daughter of Joseph Easton, and had John (3)

JOHN SKINNER (3), son of John (2) and Mary (Easton) Skinner, was born March 1, 1667 He married Rachel Pratt , died Aug 17, 1745, aged 77 They had a son Timothy

TIMOTHY SKINNER, son of John and Rachel (Pratt) Skinner, was born —— He married Ruth Colton, daughter of Rev Benjamin Colton, son of Ephraim, son of George

GEORGE COLTON, known in the record by the title of Quartermaster, is said to have come from a town in England called Sutton Cofield He settled first in Windsor, Conn , and married Deborah Gardner He removed to Hartford and was one of the first settlers of that part of Springfield, Mass , called Long Meadow He had nine children, of whom Ephraim was second

EPHRAIM COLTON, son of George and Deborah (Gardner) Colton, was born April 9, 1648 He married, first, Mary Drake, who died Oct 19 1781, second, Esther Marshfield, daughter of Samuel and Catharine Marshfield (she was born Sept 6, 1667) They had thirteen children, of whom Benjamin was the third

REV BENJAMIN COLTON, son of Ephraim and Esther (Marshfield) Colton, was born in 1690 and died 1759 He was ordained pastor of the Congregational Church in West Hartford, Feb 24, 1713, and continued his labors there till his death, March 1, 1759 He married Ruth Taylor, daughter of Rev Edward Taylor

REV EDWARD TAYLOR was born at Coventry, England, 1642, came over from Sketchley, Leicestershire, Eng , in 1668 graduated at Harvard 1671, and settled at Westfield, Mass , the same year, was ordained the day the church was organized and, as was the custom, preached his own ordination sermon He was Calvinistic in his doctrine, a man of sincere piety and exemplary behavior He had some knowledge of medicine and ministered to disease of the body as well as soul He was three times married first to Elizabeth Fitch, of Norwich, Conn , second to Ruth Wyllys, of Hartford Conn , daughter of Hon Samuel Wyllys, and to Ruth Haynes, daughter of Gov John Haynes who married Mabel Harlakenden (See Perkins, Pitkin and Woodbridge families for details of same line)

REV EDWARD TAYLOR by his wife Ruth (Wyllys) Taylor, had a daughter Ruth, who married Rev Benjamin Colton

Between the lines of Hon George Grinnell and his children, through the various marriages, there are six governors, eleven clergymen, and direct descendants of five signers of the Mayflower Compact.

Hon GEORGE GRINNELL, by Eliza Seymour (Perkins) Grinnell, his wife, had

JAMES SEYMOUR GRINNELL, b July 24, 1821, m Kate (Russell) Denison, June 19, 1879

GEORGE BLAKE GRINNELL, b November 11, 1823, m Helen Alvord Lansing December 21, 1848

HELEN ELIZA GRINNELL, b August 13, 1828; m George Milne, of England, September 6, 1847

WILLIAM FOWLER GRINNELL, b June 2, 1831 m Mary Morton, February 27, 1856

THOMAS PERKINS GRINNELL, b July 16, 1833, m E Augusta Aycrigg, December, 1859

HARRIET CAMPFIELD GRINNELL, b February 27, 1836, m Michael McCulloch, February 28, 1862

ELLA L GRINNELL, b June 19, 1839, m Thomas W. Ripley, January 29, 1868

George Blake Grinnell, son of Hon George and Eliza Seymour (Perkins) Grinnell, was born in Greenfield, Franklin County, Mass, November 11 1823 died December 19, 1891

His first knowledge of business was acquired under the instruction of his uncle, James Seymour, then engaged in the banking business at Auburn, N Y In 1843, before he reached his majority, he obtained a position with his cousin Geo Bird, a large wholesale New York dry goods house, where his business qualifications were rewarded by a partnership in the course of a few years He became a partner in 1850, and soon after the death of his cousin in 1857 he formed a copartnership with Levi P Morton (afterward Governor of the State of New York) under the firm name of Morton, Grinnell & Co, in the wholesale commission dry goods business This was one of the best known firms in the country, and continued in successful operation until the breaking out of the Civil War when the entire loss of a large Southern trade compelled the firm to suspend and settle with their creditors on a basis of thirty three and a third per cent He subsequently engaged in the banking business and was very successful In 1873, prior to the great financial panic, he called his creditors together and settled his own and his old firm's indebtedness, a balance of sixty six and two thirds cents on the dollar, with interest at seven per cent from 1861 to 1873, a period of twelve years His investments, which were largely in up town real estate, evinced great wisdom and foresight

Mr Grinnell married Helen Alvord Lansing, daughter of Rev Dirck Cornelius Lansing, son of Abraham Jacob, son of Jacob, son of Frederick

FREDERICK GERRIT LANSING, son of Frederick Lansing, of the town of Hassel, in the Province of Overyssell, came to New Amsterdam with three sons to Rennselaerwyck about 1650,

with his three daughters, he had seven children, of whom *Hendrick* was the second

HENDRICK LANSING, son of Gerrit Frederick, was born probably in Hassel He married Lysbet ———, and had five children, of whom the second was *Jacob*

JACOB LANSING, son of Hendrick and Lisbeth ——— Lansing was born about 1679, died Oct 7, 1756 He married, Sept 27 1701, Helena Pruyn, daughter of Frans Jan Pruyn

FRANCIS PRUYN or Pruen, called Frans Jansen the son of John Pruyn, was in Albany, with his wife Seltje as early as 1665 Being a Papist, he refused, in January, 1689, to take the oath of allegiance to King William, but expressed himself as willing to swear fidelity His son John, however, subscribed to the oath His wife joined the Reformed Protestant Dutch Church They had thirteen children, of whom *Helena* was the tenth She married Jacob Lansing.

JACOB LANSING, by his wife Helen (Pruyn) Lansing, had ten children, of whom *Abraham* was the ninth

ABRAHAM JACOB LANSING, ninth child of Jacob and Helena (Pruyn) Lansing, was baptized April 24, 1720 He married Catharine, daughter of Levinus Lieverse and Catryna Van der Bergh (bap March 6, 1723) He was known as the patroon He founded the present town of Lansingburg, having acquired the patent in 1767 He died Oct 14, 1791 His wife Catharina died the morning of the day before in the sixty ninth year of her age They had, besides daughters, sons Jacob A , Levinus and *Cornelius* The name of Abraham Lansing appears among the signers of the Articles of Association May 22, 1775

CORNELIUS LANSING, son of Abraham, was baptized July 6 1752, died April 23, 1842 He lived in what is now known as the Abbey property He married Hester Van Der Heyden, and had issue *Dirck Cornelius*

REV DIRCK CORNELIUS LANSING. D D , son of Cornelius and Hester (Van Der Heyden) Lansing, was born at Lansingburg N Y . March 3, 1785 He was graduated at Yale in 1804, studied theology with Rev Dr Blatchford, of Lansingburg He had seven pastorates, but the longest and with the largest success at Auburn He was the original projector of Auburn The ological Seminary, and while pastor there acted as its financial agent and raised, personally, more than $100,000 for its endowment, and filled for some time also the chair of Sacred Rhetoric in the Seminary He married Laura Alexander, daughter of Rev Caleb Alexander (She was born July 30, 1793, and died March 6, 1831)

REV CALEB ALEXANDER was born in Northfield, Mass , July 22, 1755 He was elected, July 22, 1812, the first President of Hamilton College, but did not accept He married Lucina Strong, daughter of Rev Thomas Strong and Mehitable Stebbins, and grandson of Elder Ebenezer Strong, son of Elder John Strong

Rev Dirck Cornelius Lansing, by his wife Laura (Alexander) Lansing, had issue *Helen Alvord*, who married George B Grinnell

WILLIAM FOWLER GRINNELL, son of Hon George and Eliza Seymour (Perkins) Grinnell was born in Greenfield, Franklin County, Mass , June 2, 1831 He came to New York as a boy

and for some years engaged in mercantile pursuits, being at one time partner in the firm of Morton, Grinnell & Co. Later he was a stock broker. In 1877 he was appointed by President Hayes United States Consul at St. Etienne, France, and since then has been continuously in the consular service. He has conducted with great ability and credit the consular offices at Bremen, Germany, and at Bradford and Manchester, England.

William Fowler Grinnell married February 27, 1856, Mary Morton, fifth child of Rev. Daniel Oliver, and Lucretia Parsons Morton.

GEORGE MORTON, the ancestor, was born about 1585 in Austerfield, Yorkshire, England. He married Juliana Carpenter and came to Plymouth on the Ann, early in June, 1623.

HON. JOHN MORTON, 2nd son of George, married Lettice (———) and had John.

JOHN MORTON, son of Hon. John, married Mary Ring, grand-daughter of Stephen Hopkins, of the Mayflower, and had Ebenezer.

CAPTAIN EBENEZER MORTON, fourth child of John, married Mrs. Sarah Cobb, and had a son Ebenezer.

EBENEZER MORTON, son of Capt. Ebenezer, married Mercy Foster. Their fourth child was a son, Livy.

LIVY MORTON, son of Ebenezer Morton, married Hannah Dailey.

REV. DANIEL OLIVER MORTON, son of Livy Morton, married Lucretia Parsons.

The Spencer and Allied Families.

Recent research has brought to light the fact that there were four brothers by the name of Spencer viz William, Thomas Michael and Gerrard, living in New England at the same time, and that these were the sons of Gerrard Spencer, of Stottold Bedfordshire, England The name Gerrard was a surname and no doubt derived through the marriage of one of his immediate ancestors with a Gerrard showing that he was evidently a descendant of this ancient and distinguished family.

While there may be still one or two missing links in the English line, the origin and antiquity of the Spencer family is fully established It begins with

Juan Viscount Constantine who married Ermine Sui Alini Cometes Britanie

Hudardus Dominus de Dutton, married Alicia de Dutton

Sir Hugo Dominus de Dutton

Hugh qui fuit le Despenser (Henry I, 1100 1135)

Thurston le Despenser

Americus le Despenser de Stanley, married Eldai Blewett

Thomas le Despenser

Sir Galfridus le Despenser, 1251

Collins' Peerage states that "The family of Spencers were made peers by James I, by the title of Lord Spencer of Wormleighton, and were afterwards made Earls of Sunderland, obtained the Dukedom of Marlborough by a marriage with Lady Anne, second daughter and coheir of John Churchill, the celebrated Duke of that title whose ancestry in England began with Roger de Council, eldest son of Wandril, who came into England in 1066, with William the Conqueror, and was rewarded for his services with divers lands in Somersetshire and Devonshire (as appears by the Domesday Book), part whereof was the lordship of Churchill which was anciently written Curchil, Churchel Cherchei etc, and was so denominated from being the habitation of his family '

Forty-five designs of the coat armour of the Spencer family are given in Burke's General Armory The most ancient of these is that of Baron Churchill, described as

Arms—Quarterly, first and fourth quarterly, argent and gules, in the second and third quarters a fret or, over all on a bend sable three escallops of the first   .   .

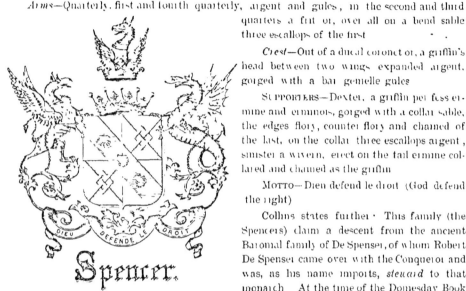

Crest—Out of a ducal coronet or, a griffin's head between two wings expanded argent, gorged with a bar gemelle gules

SUPPORTERS—Dexter, a griffin per fess ermine and erminois, gorged with a collar sable, the edges flory, counter flory and chained of the last, on the collar three escallops argent, sinister a wivern, erect on the tail ermine collared and chained as the griffin

MOTTO—Dieu defend le droit (God defend the right)

Collins states further · This family (the Spencers) claim a descent from the ancient Baronial family of De Spenser, of whom Robert De Spenser came over with the Conqueror and was, as his name imports, *steward* to that monarch   At the time of the Domesday Book he had four lordships in Warwickshire, one in Gloucestershire, fifteen in Lincolnshire and seventeen in Leicestershire

Robert Le De Spenser was father of

William De Spenser after whom was

Thurston Le De Spenser, the King's steward, a powerful man, father of Americus le Despenser de Stanley who married Eldar Blewett

Thurston Spencer, Sheriff of Gloucestershire, 19th, 20th, 22d, Henry III, who died before 1249, who by Lucia ——— left

Sir Jeffrey (or Galfridus) Spencer, who died about 1251, leaving two sons, Sir Hugh and Jeffrey   Sir Hugh, the eldest, was a great Baron and father of Hugh, Earl of Winchester, and grandfather of Hugh, Earl of Gloucester ·

Geoffrey Le De Spenser, second son, is stated to have been Lord of Marchley in Worcestershire, and to have died 1242   He was father of John Le De Spenser, who, with others of the family, took part with the Barons in their wars against Henry III   and was taken prisoner at the battle of Northampton   By Ann, his second wife, he had two sons Adam, who died young, and William

William Le Despenser left a son and heir, John Le De Spenser, who was in the retinue of John of Gaunt, nominal King of Castile, in his voyage to Spain   He was afterward Keeper of of the Wardrobe of Henry V, and was with him at the siege of Roan   He had by his wife Alice (daughter and heir of Giles Deverill),

Nicholas Spenser, whose eldest son and heir was Henry Spenser, who married Isabel, daughter and co-heir of Henry Lincoln, and had four sons, of whom the eldest was John Spenser, who had a son John

Sir John Spenser, eldest son of John, was denominated of Smithfield On Sept 3, 1506, he purchased the great lordship of Wormleighton in Co Warwick He died April 14, 1522 He married Isabel, daughter and co heir of Walter Gaunt, Esq, of Snellerfield in Warwickshire, who had issue,

Sir William Spenser, who received the honor of Knighthood A D 1529, and in 23 and 24 Henry VIII, was Sheriff of Northamptonshire He died 1532 He married Susan ——, and had

Sir John Spenser, who was Sheriff of Northamptonshire in 5 Edward VI, and elected one of the Knights of the shire in parliament for that county in the 1st Queen Mary He died Nov 8, 1586, having married Katharine, daughter of Sir Thomas Kitson, and had William

Sir William Spenser, third son of Sir John, received the honor of Knighthood from Queen Elizabeth, 1592 and died Dec 18, 1609 By his wife Margaret, daughter of Francis Bowyer, he had two sons, Thomas the eldest, and five daughters

Sir Thomas Spencer, eldest son of Sir John, was made Baron June 29, 1611, and was famous for his hospitality to the poor He died 1632 He married Margaret, daughter of Richard Bramthwait, sergeant at law, and had William

Sir William Spencer, eldest son of Sir Thomas Spencer, married Constance, daughter of Sir Thomas Lucy, of Charlecote in Warwickshire, and had Thomas

Sir Thomas Spencer, only son of Sir William Spencer, married Jane, daughter of SIR JOHN GERRARD, of Lamer in Hertfordshire, Bart Sir Thomas eldest daughter, Jane, was married to Robert Spencer, Lord Viscount of Tyrcot, of Scotland

William Spencer, who married ELIZABETH GERRARD, was the son of Sir William Spencer, 2nd Lord Spencer, and Penelope Wreothsley, daughter of Henry, Earl of Southampton

Sir William was the son of Sir Robert, 1st Lord Spencer who married Margaret Willoughby, daughter of Sir Francis

Sir Robert Spencer was the son of Sir John Spencer, ancestor of Duke of Marlborough and Earl Spencer, son of Sir John Spencer and Katharine Kitson, before mentioned

Jane Gerrard, wife of Sir Thomas Spencer, and Elizabeth Gerrard, wife of William Spencer, were descendants of Sir William Gerrard, Haberdasher, Lord Mayor of London, 1555, who married Isabel Netherell

It was probably through one of these marriages referred to that the name Gerrard came to be adopted into the Spencer family as a Christian name It was used in this form prior to the birth of Gerrard Spencer, of Stotfold, father of Gerrard Spencer, of Haddam, Conn

GERRARD FAMILY

Dominus Otho Geradine, of Florence From Italy to Normandy, thence to England, 1057 Became a favorite of Edward the Confessor, exciting jealousy of Thanes Had enormous English possessions

Walter Fitz Otho treated after the Conquest as a Norman, Castillan of Windsor and Warden of Berkshire Forest married Gladys daughter of Rhimwallon of Cynryn, Prince of North Wales

Gerald Fitz Walter Constable Pembroke Castle, married Nesta, daughter of Rhys of Grysflydd of Tudor Manor Prince of South Wales

William Fitzgerald went to Ireland with Strongbow , married Katherine Kingsley, daughter of Sir Edam

William Fitzgerald, Justice in Eyre, Co Chester

William Gerard, married daughter and heiress of Peter de Bryn

Sir Peter Gerard (time Edward III)

Sir Peter Gerard

Title wandered through several branches, and returned to his great grandson Sir Thomas, Gerard, who married Dowse Ashton, daughter of Thomas

Sir William Gerard, Haberdasher, great grandson of Thomas, was Lord Mayor of London, 1555, married Isabel Netherwell

Sir John Gerrard eldest son of Sir William, was sheriff of London 1592 Lord Mayor 1601, married Jane Partridge, daughter of Richard Partridge, Haberdasher

Sir Thomas Spencer (who married Jane Gerrard) son of Sir William son of Sir Thomas was probably the immediate ancestor of Richard Spencer, whose will forms an important connecting link between the Spencers of New England and those of Stotfold and London, England

Gerrard Spencer, of Stotfold, Bedfordshire, England, was the father of Gerrard Spencer, of Haddam, Conn, and Lynn, Mass, of Michael, of Lynn, Mass, and of William and Thomas, of Hartford, Conn While there may be one or two missing links between Gerrard Spencer and the Spencer and Gerrard families, both the name and the business- Haberdasher — (Richard, the brother of Gerrard being in that business) indicate the immediate connection of these families

Garrard.

Burke's General Armory contains the following relative to the coat armour of the Garrard family

"GARRARD Newberry, county Berks, and Dorney, county Buckingham founded by Sir William Garrard of Dorney county Buckingham, Knight, Lord Mayor of London in 1555, as was his son Sir John Garrard, Knight, in 1601 Sir John's son and heir, another Sir John Garrard, of Lamer, was raised to a baronetcy by King James I The third baronet's only daughter and heiress, Jane married Montague Drake of Shardeloes and her great grand-son, Charles Drake, inheriting the estates under the will of Sir Benet Garrard, sixth and last baronet, assumed the additional name of Garrard He was the father of Charles Benet Drake Garrard, Esq

Arms—Quarterly first and fourth argent on a fesse sable

a lion passant of the first, second and third argent a wivern with wings displayed and tail nowed gules

Crest - First a leopard sejant ppr , second a naked dexter hand and arm erect, holding a battle axe sable, headed argent

CONNECTION OF THE SPENCER FAMILIES OF CONNECTICUT WITH THE SPENCERS OF ENGLAND

The clue to the ancesters of the Spencer emigrants William, Thomas, Michael and Gerrard, was first obtained from Miss Bambridge, an industrious and enthusiastic genealogist of London, England, employed by Hon George T Spencer, of Corning, N Y, in 1868 A copy of her letter dated Aug 1, 1868, is in possession of R P Spencer of Deep River, Conn Both of these gentlemen are entitled to great credit for their indefatigable efforts in securing so much valuable and interesting data of the Spencer family

Prof Ray T Spencer while making researches in his own line discovered among the church records of St George's Parish, Stotfold, Bedfordshire, England, much interesting data, concerning the line of Gerrard Spencer, the father of William, Thomas, Michael and Gerrard the emigrants, from which it appears that the above named Gerrard was the son of Michael who also had a brother Gerrard, and they were the sons of John Thus three generations preceding the emigrants are definitely established The church records of St George's Parish, above referred to, show that "June 9, 1558, John Spencer, Sen was buried "

There is evidence to show that this John was the father of Michael and of the first Gerrard mentioned

FROM NOTES OF GEO T SPENCER

The ancestry of Gerard Spencer and his brothers William Thomas and Michael Spencer, appears from the parish registers of Edworth and Stotfeld in Bedfordshire, Eng , and other contemporaneous documents

Jan 25, 1555, Michael Spencer and Annis *Linn* were married (the last name of Annis is so poorly written in the record that it cannot be definitely determined)

April 20, 1557, John, son of Michael Spencer baptized

May 27, 1558, was baptized Michael, son of Michael Spencer

June 9, 1558, John Spencer senior was buried

April 15, 1560, buried Michael, son of Michael Spencer

21 April, 1560, John, son of Ann Spencer, widow was buried

16 June, 1560, Ann Spencer, widow, the good hospitality keeper, was buried

23 Feb , 1561, Annis, the wife of Michael Spencer was buried

20 Aug , 1564, Joan the daughter of Michael Spencer, was baptized

30 Aug , 1566, Alice, daughter of Michael Spencer was baptized, } Twins

30 Aug , 1566, Michael Spencer, was baptized,

24 July 156 , Ann, daughter of Michael Spencer baptized

30 July, 1568, Jarratt Spencer and Ellen Whiston were married, whose will was proved at London, 20 May, 1577, he was brother of Michael the elder

12 March 1571 Thomas, son of Michael Spencer, was baptized

~20 May, 1576, Gerat Spencer, son of Michael Spencer, and Elizabeth his wife, baptized

9 July, 1580, Richard, son of Michael and Elizabeth Spencer, baptized

18 Nov , 1599, Elizabeth, wife of Michael Spencer, was buried

It is quite probable that Michael Spencer of Edworth, and Gerrard Spencer of Biggleswade, were sons of John Spencer, Senior, and Ann Spencer whose burials are recorded in Edworth register, the former June 9, 1558, and the latter June 16, 1560 —Nothing more is known of them than what is disclosed by these records and the absence of further information may be accounted for by the fact that these registers do not extend back beyond 1552, and that many wills and valuable records and documents, it is said, were destroyed during the civil wars

The copies of entries in the Parish registers of Stotfold and Edgworth Beds England, were transcribed by Prof Ray T Spencer while on a visit to England in 1890-91 in search of the ancestor of the nephew of John Spencer, of Newbury, Mass , named in his will He also procured the copies of the other documents from English sources, from which citations or copies are here given including the will of Richard Spencer A part of these were published in the N E Hist and Gen Reg vols XLV and XLVI The following from the church records gives the birth of Gerrard, (father of the American emigrants), and his children

"20 May, 1576, Gerat, son of Michael Spencer and Elizabeth his wife was baptized "
His children were
"1601, Oct 11, WILLIAM SPENCER, son of Gerrard, bap
       [Moved to New England and settled in Hartford]
"1602, Oct 31, Elizabeth daughter of Gerrard, bap
"1603, Jan 22, John, son of Gerrard, bap
"1605, Aug 11, Henry, son of Gerrard bap
"1607, March 29, THOMAS, son of Gerrard bap
[Moved to New England and settled in Cambridge, Mass , moved thence to Hartford, Conn]
"1607, Oct. 20, Henry, son of Gerrard bap
"1608, Dec. 11, Richard, son of Gerrard bap   [See his will]
~"1611, May 5, MICHAEL, son of Gerrard bap
       [Moved to New England, settled in Lynn, Mass]
"1614, April 25, GERARD, son of Gerard, bap
       [Moved to New England, settled in Haddam, Ct]
"1614, May 6, Richard, son of Gerard, buried "

Gerat (or Gerrard) Spencer, the youngest child of Michael, was by his second wife, as appears by the following record

" May 2, 1576, Gerat Spencer, son of Michael and Elizabeth his wife, bap '

GERRARD SPENCER (as the name was most commonly written), son of Michael and Elizabeth (———) Spencer, was born at Stotfold, in Bedfordshire, England, May 2, 1576 He was the father of the New England emigrants, William, Thomas Michael and Gerard

The following items were copied from the English records by Prof Ray T Spencer for George T Spencer, of Corning, N Y

"Jan 20, 1615 Gerrard Spencer, the elder, gent, and Alice his wife, granted to Thomas Spencer, the elder, gent, lands in Stotfold for 99 years or during the lives of Gerrard Spencer the younger, Richard Spencer and Anthony Spencer, sons of Thomas, he paying 10s per year, and for this Thomas gave Gerrard 41 pounds

"June 25, 1616 Gerrard Spencer, of Stotfold, gent, conveyed to Thomas Spencer, of London, citizen &c certain tenements and lands in Stotfold, as security for the payment of 60 pounds, 5 acres which, it is recited, were purchased by Michael Spencer, the father of said Thomas and Gerrard

"July 24, 1617 Gerrard Spencer, of Stotfold, gent, releases and conveys absolutely the same premises to said Thomas Spencer and in the deed is repeated the recital of the land purchased by Michael Spencer, father of said Thomas and Gerrard On the same day, July 24, 1617, Gerrard Spencer of Stotfold, gent, conveyed to Thomas Spencer, citizen, of London for the consideration of 54 pounds, one half of 39 acres of land in Stotfold, and one half of two acres of meadow in Stotfold, which were granted by John Wynnes to said Gerrard Spencer and William Spencer, his son, Sept 3, 1603

"Thomas Spencer, of London, eldest son and heir of Thomas Spencer, of Stotfold, deceased, brought suit in the Court of Request against Thomas Spencer, of Stotfold, reciting that Gerrard Spencer, his uncle, seventeen years last past demised and leased to his father a house, tenement and appurtenances and seven acres of land in Stotfold This is the same lease before mentioned from Gerrard and Alice, his wife, to Thomas for 99 years "

The N E Hist and Gen Reg vols XIV and XLVI, contain the following, which is a repetition of that obtained by Hon Geo T Spencer, of Corning, N Y

Francis Spencer, of St Giles, without Cripplegate, London, citizen and brewer of London, 7 April, 1636 proved 24 Oct, 1636 My son, Thomas Spencer shall immediately, after my decease, have, hold and enjoy to him, and his heirs forever, all my houses, lands, tenements and hereditaments, etc, in Hitchin, Herts, which for the most part I have already stated to him * * and I appoint my uncle Richard Spencer, citizen and haberdasher of London, and brother Daniel Spencer, citizen and grocer of London, to be overseer

Richard Spencer, gent, 17 March, 1645, with a codicil bearing date 29 May, 1646, proved 8 June, 1646 To Thomas Spencer, son of my brother, Thomas Spencer, all my copyhold lands and tenements by me purchased of the creditors of Walter Marston, situate in Kingsbury street, near St Albans, in the county of Hertford in the parish of St Michael To Daniel Spencer, of London, grocer, son of my brother John Spencer deceased, all of those eight messuages or tenements, etc, lately by me purchased of John Gearing, grocer, * * * To Sarah Bland and Hannah Bland, daughter of my sister Katharine Bland, deceased, and to Elizabeth Tomlyns widow, daughter of my brother, Jerrard Spencer, deceased, my messuages or tenements * * * * To the said Daniel Spencer all my land and tenements in the counties of Kent and Essex, he to pay unto Anthony Spencer and Jerrard Spencer, sons of my brother Thomas Spencer, deceased, and unto two children of Margaret Spencer, deceased, now in or near London, and at the desposing of Elizabeth Carter, their aunt, the sum of thirty pounds yearly,

during their natural lives * * * and ten pounds per annum to the said two children, and ten pounds per annum to the said two children and ten pounds apiece to the said Anthony Spencer and Jerrard Spencer, to be paid unto them and to their guardians by half yearly pay ments, as the rent of said lands and tenements shall grow to after my decease

"Item I give and bequeath unto Jerrard Spencer, Thomas Spencer and Michael Spencer, sons of my brother Jarrard Spencer deceased the sum of fifty pounds apiece, and unto the children of William Spencer son of my brother, Jarrard Spencer, deceased, to be divided equally between them the sum of fifty pounds, to be paid unto their guardians, and within two years next after my decease

All of these brothers above mentioned were living in New England at the time of their uncle's death

Michael Spencer appears as owner of land in Newtown in 1634,—was made freeman in 1638, and removed to Lynn Mass, the same year   He married the widow of Thomas Robbins, of Salem   He died at Lynn in 1653, leaving two children, Susanna, born 1643, and Michael, six years old at the time of his father's death   His brother Gerard was appointed administrator of his estate

He was a legatee of his uncle Richard Spencer, of London, as appears by a Bill of Exchange drawn by him on Daniel Spencer the executor of Richard Spencer's will dated Jan 1st, 1645, at thirty days sight for thirty pounds, part of the legacy in favor of Thomas Ruck, which was given in evidence in trial in Essex County Court at Salem in 1671, between John Ruck administrator, and Joseph Armitage   *The bill had been protested for non payment*   In what way this bill of exchange was involved in the suit does not appear

Michael Spencer owned land in Hartford Conn, as appears by the land records

"Land in Hartford upon Conneckticott River belonging to Mikell Spencer and to his heirs forever"

One p sell on which his dwelling house now standeth, with other outhouses yardes and gardens thereon being wich he bought of John Bidwell contain by estima three roods be it more or les, abutting on the highway leading to the mill on the south, and on the Widow Bettes her land toward the west and on the buring place on the east, and on Seathe Grant s land on the north   " He sold this land about Feb 1646   On that date appears on the Court Records of Essex County Mass, the following

9th month, 1653, No 32   The Administrator of the estate of Mikell Spencer is granted to Gerrard Spencer of Lynn and he is to bring in an inventory of his estate the next Court '

6th of 1st mo 1653-4, No 67   Gerrard Spencer brought into this court an inventory of 22lb 40 10d of his Brother Michael Spencer and Bush ones at sea ventured and debts 10s, this court doth joyne Capt William Trask of Salem wth ye said Gerrard Spencer for the dis posing of ye estate for the bringing up of the children of ye said Michall Spencer * * * The Court doth order and agree wth the consent of Gerrard Spencer, administrator of ye estate of ye said Michall   * * In consideration of a child of the sd Michall put him to bring upp until he bee 21 years ould, wch child of name is Michall Spencer of about 6 years ould "

GERRARD SPENCER OF HADDAM, CONN., AND HIS DESCENDANTS

Gerrard or Jerrard Spencer, the founder of the Haddam and Saybrook, Connecticut, families of this name, born in Stotfold, England bap April 28, 1614, was the son of Gerrard Spencer and nephew of Sir Richard. He came to New England in 1632, and was admitted March 9, 1637, a freeman of the Massachusetts Bay Colony March 9, 1637. He was a resident of Cambridge 1634, and owned land on the south side of the river. He removed to Lynn, and at

"A Gennerall Courte houlden at Boston the 13th of the 1st Month, 1638, Garrtt Spencer is granted the ferry at Lynn for two years, taking 2d for a single pson to the furtherest place, and but 1d for a single pson to the nearest place." He was one of the Jurymen from Lynn at a County Court held the 25th of the 10th month, 1638. In 1653 he was appointed administrato on the estate of his brother Michael Spencer, who was also of Lynn. In June, 1656, he was chosen Ensign of the train band of Lynn, and in 1659 Grand Juror. He was in Connecticut the following year, as Simon Lobdell sued him and his daughter Hannah for damages because she refused to marry Lobdell

He was probably in Hartford for a short time. In 1662 he and his son John were among the 28 purchasers of the town of Haddam, which was then and for many years afterward a part of Hartford County. Barbour, in his Historical Collections of Conn., states that the tract was taken up mostly by young men from the vicinity of Hartford, who settled the northern part of this land on the west side of the river. Two of his sons were assigned home lots in the division of 1671. The records show that he was the wealthiest man in the town. He was admitted freeman of the Colony of Conn in 1672, was Ensign of the Militia, and represented the town at the General Court 1674-5, also 1678 and '79, 1680 and 81. He died in 1685, his will bearing date two years earlier

The will of Gerrard Spencer, dated Sept. 17, 1683, was admitted to probate in 1685, and is as follows

The Last Will and Testament of Jarrard Spencer, of Haddam

"In the first place it is my will that all my lawful debts shall be payd concerning my estate that God hath left me. It is my will that my sons have after the rate of twenty and my daughters fifteen. I give unto my son William that land which I bought of Stephen Laxford's estate; how I came by it the Court Records will show. I give unto my son William the third part of forty eight acres, be it more or less, lying by that which is commonly called Mills his brook; likewise I give unto my son William an acre of swamp mowing land adjoining to my house meadow lot, which particulars mentioned shall be all his part of my estate

I give to my son Nathaniel, and to his heirs, my now dwelling house in the lot with an addition lying by the side of it, granted by the committee; likewise I give my son Nathaniel one-third part of that lot formerly mentioned lying by Wells his brook; likewise I give unto my son Nathaniel an acre of swamp lying at the end of my meadow lott, and joining to his brother William formerly given; likewise I give unto my son Nathaniel forty acres, which is a third part of six score acres, and this is to be his portion

"I give unto my daughter Rebecca that house lot I bought of Thomas Smith; likewise I

give unto my daughter Rebecca one third part of that lott by Wells his brook, and this is to be her portion if she will accept it ; if not to take what falls to her in the distribution.

I give unto my son Thomas forty acres on Matchamoodus side, being part of that lot whereof his brother Nathaniel hath a share   I give unto my son Thomas his son, Jarrard Spencer, my rapier

"I give unto my son Timothy Spencer the remaynder of that six acre lot whereof his two brothers had their shares before, which six acres are those my sons shall choose   The other six acre-lot I dispose of as followeth to Grace Spencer, the daughter of my son John Spencer, forty acres, to Alice Brooke, the daughter of my daughter Brooke, forty acres, to Grace Spencer, the daughter of my son Samuel Spencer I give the other forty acres   I give unto Jarrard Cone the son of my daughter Cone, my carbine   A pewter flagon and rim bayson I give unto the church at Haddam if there be one within five years after the date hereof   It is my will that my son John his children, and my son-in-law, Daniel Cone, his children, have an equal proportion of my estate with my other children   It is my will that however my estate falls out for portion to my children that my daughter Ruth Clark's portion shall be fifteen pounds, which was my covenant with her father at her marriage, which fifteen pounds she hath received some part of it as my books will testify   One thing I forgot one feather bed which I give to my son Nathaniel

Dated Sept 17, 1683   JERRARD SPENCER
        Witness   JOHN JAMES,
                  JOSEPH ARNOLD

The children of Gerrard Spencer and Hannah, his wife were
   I   John, born at Lynn, Mass . 1638 , died Aug 3, 1682
   II   Hannah, born 1640, married Daniel Brainerd
   III. Alice, born 1641 , married, 1st Thomas Brooks 2nd Thomas Shailer.
   IV   Mehitable, born 1642   married Daniel Cone
   V   *Thomas,* married Elizabeth Bates , removed to Westbrook before 1679
   VI   Samuel
   VII   William
   VIII. Nathaniel   (?   >.
   IX.   Rebecca, married 1st John Kennard, of Haddam, about 1692 he died Feb 1689 , she married 2nd John Tanner of Lyme, Conn
   X   Ruth, married Joseph Clark
   XI   Timothy

DESCENDANTS OF THOMAS SPENCER, OF WESTBROOK, SECOND CHILD OF GERRARD AND HANNAH SPENCER

Thomas Spencer, fifth child of Gerrard and Hannah (————) Spencer, was born in Lynn, Mass probably about 1650   He removed with his parents to Haddam and may have settled in Saybrook before 1679, as his second child was born there in that year   He was voted an inhabitant Dec 8, 1687, and resided in that part of the town known as Pochaug, now West-

brook, Conn He was chosen Lister July 29, 1692, and probably held other positions in the town His inventory March 1699 1700 was appraised at £302 14 11, a large sum for those days He married Elizabeth Bates daughter of James Bates (2) of Dorchester, Mass, (bap Dec 19, 1624) and Anne, daughter of Henry Withington, of Dorchester, son of James Bates (1), of Dorchester, born at Lydd, Kent, England, 1582, came to Dorchester 1635, married Alice —— Thomas Spencer, by his wife Elizabeth (Bates) Spencer, had issue .

Jarrard, born Oct 8, 1673 at Haddam, bap at Middletown, July 5, 1674 5—his parents were members of the church at Lynn

Thomas, born April 1, 1679, at Saybrook

Caleb, born Jan 19, 1695 6, at Saybrook

The History of Middlesex County, page 506, referring to the "Iron Works" located in the Pond Meadow district, says "The Spencers were the last proprietors in the early part of the present century and it is altogether probable that Thomas Spencer, who settled near by, discovered the mine and founded the works prior to 1700 In 1702 the General Assembly excused Charles Williams, of Saybrook, from training he being chief workman in the iron works there and living six or seven miles from town "

"The establishment combined a smelting furnace where the metal was reduced from the ore, and a blacksmith shop where every kind of hammered work in use at that time, from a horse nail to an anvil or anchor, was made The ore was obtained from 'Mine Swamp,' but a little distance off, and the present appearance of the mining grounds, and the large quantity of slag that remains at the site of the works, leave no doubt of its importance to a large section at one time "

Caleb Spencer, youngest son of Thomas and Elizabeth (Bates) Spencer, was born in the parish of Westbrook, town of Saybrook June 19 1695 6, He was commissioned Ensign of the Train Band, and was chosen Surveyor of Highways Dec 12, 1732 He was a man of considerable means and owned several slaves, which he divided among his children at his death His slave "Toby and wife Jude, a worthy couple were received into the church ⁓ ✝ ᴹ Toby had a number of children, all born in slavery " In his will Caleb says "I give my negro man Toby to be equally divided between my three sons, Joseph, Caleb and John " By his wife Hannah (———) Caleb Spencer (1) had issue

I   *Joseph,* born April 18, 1720

II   Mary, born Sept 19, 1721

III   *Caleb* (2), born Dec 8, 1724

IV   Hannah, born Feb 13, 1727

V   Lemuel, born March 14, 1728-9, died March 30, 1729

VI   John, born Feb 11, 1730

VII   Sarah born Feb 21, 1731

VIII   Jemima, born Aug 3 1734, married Henry L Hommedieu, of Westbrook parish, Saybrook

Caleb Spencer married, second, Temperance Wright, by whom he had no issue

Joseph Spencer, eldest child of Caleb (1) and (Hannah) Spencer, was born in Westbrook Parish, April 18, 1720. He is not referred to particularly in the records and probably spent his life in the cultivation of his farm. He married Lydia Grinnell (born Aug. 28, 1713) daughter of Paybodie and Ruth (Nettleton) Grinnell.

Pabodie Grinnell was the son of Daniel (3), son of Daniel (2), son of Daniel (1), son of Matthew.

Matthew Grinnell was probably of Huguenot origin. He was among the earliest settlers of Newport, R. I., and was admitted freeman in 1638. Of his early history little is known, but the fact that among his descendents are found some of the most distinguished men of the country, indicates that he was a man of more than ordinary ability, and that he came of an excellent family. He married Rose ——. The children named in his will are Matthew, Thomas and *Daniel* (1)

Daniel Grinnell (1), son of Matthew and Rose (—— ——) Grinnell, was born about 1636. He married Mary Wodell (born 1640), daughter of William and Mary Wodell. They lived at Portsmouth and Little Compton, R. I. They had issue *Daniel*, Richard and Jonathan.

Daniel Grinnell (2), son of Daniel (1) and Mary (Wodell) Grinnell, was born at Little Compton, R. I. about 1665. He evidently did not mingle much in public affairs as his name is seldom found in the records. Extreme modesty, combined with great executive ability appears to have been characteristic of this family. He was probably a successful, thrifty farmer and devoted his whole attention to the cultivation of the ground. He removed to Saybrook, Conn., probably before 1700, and settled in Pochaug near Westbrook. His social status is shown in the distinguished family that he became allied with. He married Lydia Pabodie, daughter of William Pabodie (2), son of William (1)

[For record of Daniel Grinnell, William Pabodie, John Alden, etc. See "Grinnell and Allied Families," page 32].

Daniel Grennell (2), by his wife Lydia (Pabodie) Grinnell, had Priscilla, born 1689. *Paybodie* of Westbrook, born 1691. *Mary* married Robert Lay, of Saybrook.

This name of Paybodie, is said to have had its origin about A. D. 61, in the reign of Nero, the tyrant emperor, at which time the Ancient Britons, who were tribes of the more ancient Cambri, were in a state of vassalage to the emperor. Paisugatus, in the right of Queen Boadicia his wife, was reigning King in Icena, Briton, and hoping to secure his family and part of his immense estate in his will he gave one-half the estate to Nero, but to no purpose, for no sooner was the King dead than the officers of Nero seized everything in their power. Queen Boadicia being a woman of great abilities and power opposed these proceedings, for which Nero ordered her to be publicly whipped and her daughters submitted to the vilest insults. This so enraged the Britons that the Queen revolted, and with the assistance of her kinsman a patriarch in one of the tribes, named Boadie, put himself at the head of the Britons, fought many desperate battles with various success, made a great massacre among the Romans and would have expelled them had not Suetoneus Paulinus at the critical moment with ten thousand fresh troops, joined the Romans. The battle continued with great vigor, and the result was doubtful, till the

last victory inclined to the Romans Upon which the Queen, who had behaved with surprising bravery, determined not to submit to the tyrant dispatched herself with poison leaving Boadie to his fate, who with his men sustained the horrid massacre in a desperate manner, selling their lives for a high price to the Romans, till their numbers were reduced to a few, when Boadie, after avenging himself by killing Galbuta, a Roman officer, and taking his helmet and armor, with a remnant of Britons, escaped and took asylum over the craggy mountains of Wales, whence they made frequent excursions upon their neighbors in the low country, the Romans having reduced a great part of the island to a state of servitude Upon the helmet and armour was a Roman badge of honor and distinction described as

Arms—Party per fesse nebule, gules, azure, two suns ppr with a garb

Motto—Murus aenas conscientia sana (A sound conscience is a wall of brass)

There was also a miniature likeness of the Empress Popia, wife of Nero The Roman badge was sacredly preserved by the patriarchs of the name of Boadie as a trophy of honor

Boadie, among the ancient Cambri, afterwards Britons, signified *Man*, "or a great Man," and Pea signified a large hill or mountain, which afterwards occasioned this patriarch leader to be called and distinguished among the neighboring enemy by the name of PEABODIE or MOUNTAIN MAN This tribe multiplied considerably, and some of them by tilling the land, a part of which was fertile, became very opulent, but most of them remained in a rude state Some of them were herdsmen and kept cattle, others supported themselves by ranging the forest, &c, having many bloody conflicts with their neighbors, which often reduced their numbers and kept them in great distress, until, in the sixth century, when they were so far reduced that a compromise took place, after which they began to assimilate to their neighbors In the reign of King Arthur, the Kingdom being invaded by the northern Saxons and others, a leader, or patriarch of the tribes by the name of Peabodie, a man of much influence and wealth, by his prowess and exertions in the battle on the river Douglass, aided much in expelling the invaders, and having in his possession the trophy that had been taken from the Romans, and carefully preserved by his ancestor—the reigning King Arthur, as a reward for his unshaken fidelity and heroic valor, ordered it to be registered, with additions, so as to stand as above stated to the name of Peabodie While some of the name and family kept the name of Boadie—which with some was afterwards anglicized, when the name of Man while others kept the name of Pea which being also anglicized some were called Hill others Mont and Mountain Hence these names, and there are arms to each name, but none so ancient

Extracted from the Ancient Records Vol II Folio 327, No 109, and transferred to Modern Records, Vol II, Folio 65, No 97

Signed   ROBLTT N ANDREWS, Ass't Secty

Examined   B GERARD, Armorer

Fees £2, 2, 0

Heraldry Office London, Cheapside, Oct 23, 1796

Reg. les Francis Peabody, who has numerous descendants, there was also John Paybody, who was one of the original proprietors of Bridgewater, Mass, in 1645, and was representative at Plymouth in 1645, there was also a WILLIAM PABODIE, who signed himself PABODIE

Paybodie Grinnell, second child and oldest son of Daniel (3) and Lydia (Pabodie) Grinnell, was born in 1694. He moved to Pochauge (Westbrook) in the old town of Saybrook, probably about 1720. His name appears on the list of those who responded to the call of the Assembly for troops in the expedition against Canada.

"An account of what was Delivered out of Saybrook Town Stock of ammunition to Capt James Harris's Company, Sept 12th and 13th per me John Tully."

"Paybody Grinnell 1 lb of Powder."

Paybody Grinnell married Ruth Nettleton (born about 1693), and had issue *Lydia*, who was married to Joseph Spencer.

Joseph Spencer (1) by his wife Lydia (Grinnell) Spencer had issue

    I   Joseph (2) born Aug 12, 1744

    II   Daniel born Feb 2, 1746, married Temperance Dowd January 17, 1770, died May 16, 1806

    III Lydia born Feb 22, 1748, married 1st Elisha Pratt, 2nd Joseph Stannard, died April 7, 1801

    IV Ruth, born Feb 2, 1750 married Nathaniel Post Dec 21 1765, died Sept 27, 1782

    V   Hannah, born Jan 31, 1753, married 1st Samuel Wright March 22, 1755, 2nd Noah Platts

    VI George, born June 17, 1755

    VII Mary, born Jan 11, 1757, married John Wright July 19, 1751 (?)

    VIII Nabby, born May 4, 1761, died March 26, 1764

    IX Peter, born Aug 31, 1763, married 1st Jerusha Post April 3, 1785, 2nd Lucretia Ruggles, 1804, 3d Jerusha Buckley April 12, 1810

    X   Phebe, born May 26, 1767, married ——— Turner

Joseph Spencer (2), son of Joseph (1) and Lydia (Grinnell) Spencer, was born in the parish of Westbrook town of Saybrook Aug 12 1744. He was twice married. His first wife was Elizabeth (born April 9, 1748) daughter of John and Elizabeth (Williams) Clark whom he married 2nd Nov, 1769, she died June 25, 1777, he married 2nd, Lucy, daughter of Benjamin Post and Mary (Colt) Post, July 5, 1780, (she was born June 4, 1746, died 11 Jan, 1834) He died Nov 15, 1793. Joseph Spencer had issue by his first wife:

    I   Nabby Spencer, born Jan 14, 1770, died Jan 6, 1843; married Beaumont Clark, he died Oct 5, 1857

    II   Elizabeth Spencer, born March 26, 1772, married June 3, 1796, Nathan Pratt, of Potapogue—now Essex, Conn He died Feb 22, 1842, she died Feb 17, 1847

    III Hester Spencer, born June 24, 1777 married Simeon Abell He removed to Chataqua Co N Y, living in Syracuse 1840

Children by second wife

    IV. *Joseph Spencer* born May 1, 1781, married Saba Dee Sept 20, 1801, died Nov 25, 1852

    V. Ezra Spencer, born Dec 29, 1782, married 1st, Melntable Bushnell, 2nd Eliza Clark He died Jan 7, 1864, at Mt Pleasant, Pa, whence he removed in 1846

VI   *David Spencer*, born Dec 16, 1785 married Rachel Bushnell

VII   *George Spencer* born Oct 6, 1787, married 1st, Julia Pratt, 2nd Ursula Read, 3d
      Anne E Bates

VIII Lucy Spencer, born Sept 6 1789, died Oct 31, 1793

DESCENDANTS OF DAVID SPENCER, SIXTH CHILD OF JOSEPH (2) AND LUCY POST SPENCER

David Spencer, third child of Joseph (2) and Lucy (Post) Spencer, was born Dec 16
1785, in that part of the old town of Saybrook known as Westbrook   He was an industrious,
thrifty farmer, and combined with farming the occupations of mason and blacksmith two
trades very essential in a sparsely settled community   He was a very helpful man among his
neighbors, and much respected and honored for his many personal qualities   Upright, honest
and public spirited, he made the most of his surroundings

He married Rachel daughter of Asa Bushnell and Hannah Chapman, daughter of Ichabod
son of Nathaniel (2), son of Deacon Nathaniel, son of Robert Chapman the ancestor of the Saybrook and East Haddam branches of the Chapman family

The name Chapman derives from the Saxon word Cheapman, meaning a merchant or
cheapner

Robert Chapman, the ancestor of the Saybrook branch of the family, was born in 1616,
came from Hull, England to Boston in 1635, and on Nov 3, following, he sailed from there in
company with Lion Gardiner for Saybrook, Conn   as one of the company of twenty men who
were sent by Sir Richard Saltonstall to take possession of a large tract of land near the mouth
of the Connecticut river   He helped to subdue the Indians taking an active part in company
with his particular friend, Col George Fenwick   in the various Indian warfares incident to the
early settlement of Connecticut, and especially in the Pequot War   He was a large landholder
in the towns of Saybrook and East Haddam   He also owned a large tract of land in Hebron,
and left at his decease to each of his three sons fifteen hundred acres in that town which he received as one of the legatees of the Indian Chief Uncas and his sons   He settled himself on a
tract of land in Oyster River, about two miles west of Saybrook fort and this homestead is still
in the possession of his descendants   He was a leading man in the town and much engaged in
public affairs   He was for many years town clerk and commissioner for Saybrook, and represented the town as Deputy to the General Court forty-five times, and was Governor's Assistant
nine times   He died October 13 1687   He married Anne Blith (or Bliss) April 29, 1642, and
had issue, John, Robert, Anna, Hannah *Nathaniel* (1), Mary, Sarah

Deacon Nathaniel Chapman fifth child of Robert was born Feb 16, 1653   He was for
many years a deacon of the church in Saybrook, and represented the town at the General Court
of Connecticut twenty four sessions—1697 to 1723   He was a very large landholder, as appears
from the records of the town of Saybrook and of the Oyster River Quarter   He owned fifteen
hundred acres of land in Hebron, which he received by inheritance from his father, and presented to his son the Rev Daniel Chapman   On the decease of his father he inherited the
paternal homestead and left the same by will to his youngest son Caleb   He married, June
29, 1681, Mary Collins, of Guilford, daughter of John Collins   He married 2nd, Hannah Bates

By his first wife he had Nathaniel, died soon   Nathaniel (2), born July 19, 1686, David, 1689, and John   By his second wife he had Mary Hannah, Phineas Caleb, Anne

Nathaniel Chapman (2), son of Deacon Nathaniel and Mary (Collins) Chapman, was born July 19, 1686   He resided in what is now Westbrook, about half a mile east of the Congregational Meeting house   He married, Aug 1709, Elizabeth Spencer, and had issue, *Ichabod* and Nathaniel (3)

Ichabod Chapman, eldest child of Nathaniel (2) and Elizabeth (Spencer) Chapman, was born in Westbrook, Oct 10, 1710   He was twice married, 1st to Rachel Dibble, by whom he had three children 2nd to Hannah Jones Jan 20, 1742   By his first wife he had Daniel, Elizabeth (1), Elizabeth (2)   By his second wife he had Rachel, William, Jeremiah, Ezra, *Hannah* Daniel

Hannah Chapman fifth child of Ichabod and Hannah (Jones) Chapman, was born March 20, 1751 , she was married to Asa Bushnell, whose daughter Rachel became the wife of David Spencer

David Spencer, of Saybrook, by his wife Rachel (Bushnell) Spencer had issue :

    I   *David Spencer*, born July 24, 1808, died Aug 18, 1857

    II   Nancy Spencer, born Oct 19, 1810 , died Aug 8, 1882

    III   Charles Chauncey Spencer, born Jan 8, 1813 , died Sept 6, 1876

    IV   Una Maria Spencer, born Oct 27, 1814 , died Sept 2, 1896

    V   Edwin Spencer, born Jan 12, 1817 ; died Sept 12, 1882

    VI   Alvin Benjamin Spencer, born Feb 1, 1819 · died Feb 22, 1856

    VII   Julia Elizabeth Spencer, born Oct 10, 1821

    VIII   *Daniel Chapman Spencer*, born Dec 3, 1823 , see record

    IX   Harriet Amelia Spencer, born Dec 21, 1825 , died Jan 9, 1852

    X   Emily Ann Spencer, born May 5, 1828 , died June 28, 1895

    XI   Mary Augusta Spencer, born Aug 10, 1832 , died Oct 11, 1900

David Spencer, Jr., eldest child of David and Rachel (Bushnell) Spencer, was born July 24, 1808, at Saybrook, died Aug 18, 1857, he married Emeline Chalker, April 16, 1837, she died Feb 27, 1866   They had

    I   Albert Marshall Spencer, date of birth unknown, died at Saybrook Dec 16, 1865

    II   Richard Ingham Spencer, drowned date unknown

Nancy Spencer, second child of David and Rachel (Bushnell) Spencer, was born at Saybrook, Oct 19, 1810, died there Aug 8, 1882 , married at Saybrook, Nov 27, 1834, Albert Chalker (born there Jan 30, 1808 died there May 11, 1895)   They had issue

    I   Emma Augusta Chalker born at Saybrook Dec 7, 1843 married there Jan 4, 1876, James Burnham Lord   They had issue

           1   Cornelia Hayden Lord, born Saybrook, March 20, 1878

           2   Jennie Augusta Lord, born Saybrook, March 24, 1881

           3   Albert Chalker Lord, born Saybrook, May 1, 1882

    II   Jane Elizabeth Chalker, born at Saybrook, March 7, 1847 , died March 27, 1849

CHARLES CHAUNCEY SPENCER, third child of David and Rachel (Bushnell) Spencer, was born at Saybrook, Jan 8, 1813, died there Sept 6, 1876 He married Jun 7, 1838, Lucretia Minor Harvey, born at Lyme, Conn , Feb 25, 1814, died Oct 20, 1890 They had issue   -

I Maria Adelaide, born Nov 11, 1838, married at Deep River, Oct 16, 1860, Merritt Shaler Brooks, of Chester, Conn They had,

1 Hilton Cook Brooks born in Chester, Conn, Sept 21, 1861, married in Riverton Conn , Oct 12, 1887, Winnie Gallup (born in Brooklyn, N Y , Oct 9, 1867) Their children were Lewis Merritt Brooks, born in Chester, Feb 7, 1889, Marjori Cristobel Brooks, born in Chester, June 12, 1891 , Malcolm Gallup Brooks, born in Chester, Dec 12, 1893

2 Jessie Brooks, born in Chester, Feb 21, 1863 , died in Saybrook, Aug 30, 1878

3 Simeon Spencer Brooks, born in Chester, Nov 17, 1865 , he married at Clinton, Conn Sept 26, 1888, Mary Josephine Beckley Wright, born in Clinton, Conn , Nov 22, 1869, and had Florence Brooks, born in Chester, Oct 21, 1889

4 Agnes Brooks, born in Chester, June 6, 1871, died there Dec 24, 1882

II Frances Catharine, second child of Charles Chauncey Spencer and Lucretia Minor (Harvey) Spencer, was born May 10, 1840, married at Old Saybrook, Charles Henry Curtis, of Birmingham, Conn , July 16, 1868, he was born at Huntington, Nov 11, 1837 They had

1 Edith Maria Curtis, born in Saybrook, Sept 5, 1869 , died in Detroit, Mich , March 6, 1877

2 Bessie Margaret Curtis, born in Detroit, Oct 13, 1870

3 Fanny Eddy Spencer Curtis, born in Detroit, Oct 2, 1875

III Amelia Annette, third child of Charles Chauncey Spencer and Lucretia Minor (Harvey) Spencer, was born in Saybrook , died at Plainfield, N J , May 7, 1858

IV Mary Edgar Spencer, born in Saybrook, April 15, 1843 , married Dec 25, 1872, Samuel Hart Pratt (born in Saybrook, Aug 19, 1843) Their children were,

1 Gilbert Pratt, born in Old Saybrook, March 28, 1874

2 Sarah Pratt, born in Old Saybrook, Jan 11, 1877

3 Edith Spencer Pratt, born in Old Saybrook, Dec 23, 1879

V. Margaret Nichols Spencer, born Nov 3, 1844 , died in Deep River, Conn , Oct 12, 1859

VI Charles Samuel Spencer, born in Saybrook, Sept 15, 1846 ; married in Iowa, Jan 5, 1870, Isaphene Wood They had,

1 Edgar Fred Spencer, born in Iowa, Nov 26, 1871, married in Laporte, Ind , Dec 24, 1893, Orpha Leonore Morgan, born in Des Moines, Iowa, Sept 1, 1873 They had Ruth Isaphene, born in Monmouth, Ill , Jan 31, 1894, and Charles Hiram, born in Monmouth, Ill , June 13, 1896, Edgar Harry, born in Wheaton, Ill , June 25, 1897

2 George Allen Spencer, born May 10, 1873 , married Rebecca Pearl Eviland,

of Knoxville, Iowa, June 6, 1897; born Sept 20, 1878, in Knoxville, Iowa   They had an infant born in Knoxville, Iowa, May 22, 1898; died May 23, that year

     3   Infant daughter, no date

     4   Edna E Spencer, born Feb 14, 1877, died May, 1898

     5   Sarah, died in infancy } twins born March 19, 1881
     6   Susie, died in infancy }

     7   Blanche Spencer, born Nov 10, 1882

     8   Charles Spencer, born March 7 1885

     9   Helen Maria Spencer, born Feb 22, 1889

VII   Lucretia Marsylvia Spencer, born in Saybrook, Sept 16, 1845; married in Chicago, Ill, July 10, 1890, Alonzo Delano Bradley   No issue

VIII   Sarah Elizabeth Spencer, born in Saybrook, Nov 5, 1852, died in Brooklyn, N Y, Dec 11, 1887; married in Old Saybrook, Nov 19, 1873, to Charles William Prankard, of Brooklyn   Their children were

     1   William Spencer Prankard, born in Brooklyn, Sept 21, 1874, married, New York, Feb 16, 1898, Clara Louise Miller (born in New York City, Jan 20, 1874)

     2   Mary Arlington Prankard born in Brooklyn Feb 14, 1878

     3   Rhys Spencer Prankard born in Brooklyn, N Y, Nov 23, 1887

IX   Susan Ella Harvey Spencer, born in Deep River, Conn, July 17, 1854, died in Brooklyn, Dec 2, 1891, unmarried

USA MARIA SPENCER, fourth child of David and Rachel (Bushnell) Spencer, was born in Saybrook, Oct 27, 1814, died in Westbrook, Conn, Sept 2, 1896, married in Saybrook, Aug 8, 1847, Nathaniel C Dee   Issue

I   Alice M Dee, born in Westbrook, June 17, 1848, died there Oct 20, 1878

II   Jennie L Dee, born in Westbrook, Dec 24, 1851, died there Jan 13, 1852

III   Emily P Dee, born in Westbrook, Oct 26, 1853, married Nov 30, 1886, to John O Hayden   They had,

     1   Hattie F Hayden, born in Westbrook, Sept 14, 1887

     2   Robert S Hayden, born in Westbrook, Oct 12, 1889

     3   John O Hayden, born in Westbrook, Aug 4, 1891

IV   Ella J Dee, born in Westbrook, Aug 6, 1855, married there, Feb 12, 1878, Charles E Chapman   They had issue

     1   George S Chapman, born Nov 19, 1878

     2   Alice M Chapman, born Feb 22, 1880

     3   Joseph F Chapman, born March 24, 1882

     4.   Raymond Chapman, born March 19, 1884

     5   Amy D Chapman, born Jan 24, 1886

     6   Charles Chapman, born June 23, 1888

     7   Wilda Chapman, born Oct 29, 1889

     8.   Robert D Chapman, born April 17, 1891

     9   Ruth E Chapman, born Oct 28, 1893

EDWIN SPENCER, fifth child of David and Rachel (Bushnell) Spencer, was born in Saybrook, Jan 12, 1817, died there Sept 12, 1882, married there, April 13, 1846 Anna Augusta Chalker (born Oct 27, 1824, died June 6, 1867) They had,

I George Edwin Spencer, born in Saybrook, Sept 19, 1855, married in Old Saybrook, May 1, 1882, Annie E Jobson (born in Rhinebeck, N Y, Oct 3, 1865) They had issue Edwin V Spencer, born May 19, 1885, in Old Saybrook, and Hury P Spencer, born Feb 10, 1891

II Jane Spencer, born July 19, 1861, died Oct 9, 1861

Edwin Spencer, above mentioned, married 2nd, Jan 4, 1871, Lydia C Beers (born Sept 8, 1835, died April 19, 1894), no issue

ALVIN BENJAMIN SPENCER, sixth child of David and Rachel (Bushnell) Spencer, was born Feb 1, 1819, died at Deep River, Conn, Feb 22, 1856 He married in Essex, Conn, March 20 1842, Hannah Williams (born in Essex, Feb 13, 1820 died in Chester, Conn, Dec 16, 1891) They had issue

I Sarah C Spencer, born Feb 4, 1843, died in Deep River, Conn, June 25, 1887, married July 16, 1861, in Deep River, Frederick William Chapman, Jr (born in Hartford, Conn, May 21, 1838, died in Deep River, Sept 17 1865) Their child was Emily Williams Chapman, born in Deep River, Feb 26, 1865

Sarah C Chapman married 2nd, William A Bulkley, of Deep River, May 19, 1874 No issue

II Victorine A Spencer, born Oct 24, 1846, in Deep River, married Nov 4, 1867, at Deep River, Henry A Chapman (born in Deep River, Sept 1, 1845 They had one child, Wilfred Alvin Chapman, born in Hartford Nov 15, 1882

III Mary H Spencer, born in Deep River, Sept 9, 1850, died in Chester, Dec 24, 1891, married May 15, 1869, Adelbert W Kenyon, of Essex, Conn (born Jan 25, 1845), no issue

JULIA ELIZABETH SPENCER, seventh child of David and Rachel (Bushnell) Spencer, was born Oct 10, 1821, at Saybrook married there 1842, George Edwin Kirtland He died in Saybrook, 1857 They had issue.

I George Spencer Kirtland, born in Saybrook, Dec 23 1842; died Oct 1849

II Edward Shipman Kirtland, born in Saybrook, April 24, 1845, died Oct 1849.

III Julia Elizabeth Kirtland, born Feb 4, 1847, married in Saybrook, Oct 1880, John Henry Tileston Their children were

1 Bessie Tileston, born in Saybrook, Dec 4, 1881

2 Ruth Tileston, born in Saybrook, Nov 21, 1885

IV George Edward Kirtland, born March 28, 1849, married 1873, in Cleveland, Ohio, Elizabeth Burns (born in Scotland) Their children were

1. Frederick Woodbridge Kirtland, born 1876; died 1878

2 Lizzie Kirtland, born Sept 21, 1878

3 Mattie Kirtland, born June 25, 1882

4 Hattie Kirtland, born June 28, 1885

5 Julia Kirtland, born Aug 19, 1888

V   Harriet Spencer Kirtland born June 28, 1852, in Saybrook married there, 1876, George Washington Parker   Their children were

    1   Amy Hart Parker,   ) twins born in Saybrook, 1876

    2   Arthur Reed Parker,) He married, July 11, 1898, at Springfield, Mass , Julia Le Revere, and had issue Ruth Parker, born in Springfield, Mass , July 17, 1899

    3   Edith Merrell Parker, born in Springfield, Mass , March 31, 1883

    4   George Kirtland Parker, born in Springfield, Oct 4, 1890

VI   Franklin Joseph Kirtland born Oct 31, 1854 , married in Saybrook, 1879, Lily Mann (died there March, 1895)   They had issue

    1   Edwin Mortimer Kirtland, born in Saybrook, April 11, 1880

    2   Franklin Joseph Kirtland, Jr , born in Saybrook, Aug 30, 1881

    3   Harry Ellsworth Kirtland, born in Saybrook, Nov 1883

    4   Linda Elizabeth Kirtland born in Saybrook, March 6, 1889

    5   George Edwin Kirtland born in Saybrook, Sept 1, 1891

VII   Arthur Leslie Kirtland,   ) twins born May, 1857 , died 1873

VIII   Edwin Latimer Kirtland,)   "   "   "   "   died Aug 1857

Daniel Chapman Spencer, eighth child and fifth son of David and Rachel (Bushnell) Spencer, was born in the Oyster River quarter of the old town of Saybrook, Dec 3, 1823   Like most boys of his age, at that period, he had very little time for "schooling," as his services were required on the farm, and before he had mastered the simplest elementary branches he was, like the famous Cincinnatus, following the plow   During the winter months however, he attended the academy and acquired a fair education, sufficient, as he thought, for the inherited occupation of farming   He had already attained his majority when a little incident changed the whole current of his life and the simple farmer boy became a prominent New York merchant   While working in the field one day he had a sun stroke, which so affected his constitution that he was compelled to quit the farm and go as clerk in a country store   From a clerk in a country store he became a traveling salesman for a New Haven house   He developed a remarkable capacity for selling goods and soon acquired a reputation that extended beyond the precincts of his own state   A large wholesale dry goods firm of New York had learned of his successful career as a salesman and submitted a proposition to enter their employ   It was so startling to him that he thought they must have greatly overrated his abilities   So anxious was this firm, Messrs Moulton, Plympton, Williams & Co , to secure his services, that they gave him a check to pay for the unexpired time due to his old employers   Mr Spencer was at once placed in charge of their fancy goods department and was successful in its management up to the time of the failure of the firm   What seemed for the time to be a misfortune was indeed a blessing in disguise, for through the influence of Mr Moulton he was introduced under the most favorable conditions to the house of Claflin, Mellen & Co later H B Claflin & Co , who at that time contemplated opening a notion department in addition to their

M. C. SPENCER

large dry goods business. So sanguine was Mr. Spencer of his ability to successfully conduct this department that he offered to take charge of it for a year without any compensation. Mr. Claflin insisted however on paying him a liberal salary, with the promise of an additional amount should the venture prove a success. The firm at that time occupied the old Trinity Building on lower Broadway, and so limited were the facilities that only the basement of the building could be used for the new line of goods. Mr. Spencer, however, utilized every inch of space, bought and sold the goods and managed the business in every way as if it were his own. The result exceeded the most sanguine expectations of the firm, who showed their appreciation of his efforts by presenting him with a check at the end of the year for $1,000 in addition to his salary. In renewing their engagement with Mr. Spencer they offered him a share of the profits which was virtually equivalent to a partnership. The business of the firm increased to that extent that they were obliged to seek for larger quarters with greatly increased facilities, and they purchased a site on the corner of Church and Worth streets, running through to West Broadway, covering nearly an acre of ground. On this they erected a building six stories high, fitted up with the best facilities that could be devised. As for Mr. Spencer, he was provided with the very best accommodations for the extensive business which he had established. His department covered a large portion of the third floor and a part of the fifth floor, requiring the assistance of over forty clerks. It was a great task for one man to control and attend personally to all the details of an immense business like this, but Mr. Spencer was equal to it and the firm of Claflin, Mellen & Co. soon became from the second largest to the largest wholesale dry goods establishment in the United States, doing a business of several millions annually in excess of its famous rival. That Mr. Spencer contributed materially to this result goes without saying. During his thirteen years' connection with this house his individuality was merged into that of the firm. That Mr. Spencer helped to lay the fortunes of this great firm is acknowledged by all who are familiar with his connection with it. In the accomplishment of this almost unprecedented success Mr. Spencer overtaxed his energies and his powers of endurance, and in 1867 he was compelled to dissolve his connection with the firm and recuperate his wasted energies. He was strongly urged by Mr. Claflin to remain in the business and take ample time for rest, but Mr. Spencer felt that he had reached the climax of physical and mental endurance and that if he would prolong his life he must lay aside all the cares and responsibilities of active business. Subsequent events have shown the wisdom of his course, for more than thirty years have been added to his long, useful life, in which he has contributed much to the welfare and happiness of others. While his name may not have been emblazoned on the pages of history as one of the great merchants of the metropolis it was certainly written on the hearts of his associates and his memory will be kept green by those who knew and loved him. The thought of severing his connection with those who had been so long associated with him was one of the greatest trials of his life, but the event that followed immediately his decision was made known more than compensated for the sorrow he felt at parting and sweetened all the remaining years of his life. The account of this was described in the *New York Tribune* of Feb. 8, 1868, as follows:

"Mr. D. C. Spencer, for many years past the genial and able manager of the Fancy Goods De-

partment of the well known house of H B Claflin & Co, having been obliged on account of ill health, to retire from business, his late employes headed by his worthy and efficient successor, Mr James H Day, presented Mr Spencer with a superb silver service, of the richest yet most chaste workmanship, contained in a truly elegant black walnut casket Each piece of the service bears the following inscription

PRESENTED TO

D C SPENCER

BY HIS LATE EMPLOYEES

ON HIS RETIRING FROM BUSINESS

JAN 1, 1868

" Accompanying the service was a very handsome card, 36 by 40 inches, incased in a heavy gilt frame, on which is a photograph of the house of Claflin & Co, and one of each of the donors In the center of this card, in an oval space surrounded by the photographs, are these words

" ' We, whose familiar faces surround this Card of Presentation, would respectfully state that in your retirement from business and our midst we feel that we lose a genial face, a good counseling friend, an exemplary Christian and a true business man

" ' Expressive of our feelings of high respect for you and our deep regret that your impaired health compels our separation, we ask that you receive this Card and Service in the spirit in which it is presented, as a memento of past pleasant associations

" ' We would further add that it shall be our earnest prayer that your health may be restored and that you may long be spared to your family and for society's good '

" To these costly testimonials of the regard of his late employees and their regret at losing him from their midst, Mr Spencer replied in the following characteristic and appropriate letter

" ' GENTLEMEN —No language however eloquent, can picture the surprise and pleasure awakened in my breast by the elegant present of which you have made me the recipient, and which I shall prize most highly for its intrinsic worth, and far more as being a testimonial of your regard and esteem for me and of the pleasure and benefit you have derived from our business relations

" ' When the heart is full, many words seem but to weaken the expression of our gratitude I will only say, therefore, that for your handsome gift, and the accompanying kind wishes in my behalf, I thank you from the bottom of a grateful heart

" ' It has not been without sincere regret on my part that I have ended our business connections by withdrawing myself from your midst, but although the state of my health has rendered that withdrawal necessary, I shall ever treasure up in my mind the many pleasant memories arising from our past relations, and not one of your faces shall ever cease to be remembered with feelings of the deepest interest I shall always pray earnestly and hopefully that none of those faces may be overcast by clouds of sorrow or disappointment, but that each one of your lives may be crowned with success and happiness '

" This happy affair will long be remembered both by the recipient and the donors, and the recollection of it will doubtless be a source of great pleasure to them in after years '

After closing up his business affairs Mr Spencer returned to the home of his childhood, where he soon found sufficient employment to occupy his time. He improved and enlarged the place, purchasing a number of acres adjoining the homestead. With his practical business knowledge and with ample means at his command he soon made the old farm present a different aspect. With delightful surroundings and his mind at ease, Mr Spencer soon recovered his health. To restore the prestige of the old Saybrook Colony by making it an attractive summer resort, occupied his attention for the next few years. He purchased two acres of land at Guard House Point, and later, in connection with others, bought 250 acres of the Lynde farm. This was mostly disposed of to the New Saybrook Company and laid out in villa plots on which were erected beautiful summer residences. Mr Spencer became personally interested and was one of the promoters in all these public improvements, which included the famous hotel known as Fenwick Hall.

He was one of the promoters of the Valley Railroad and was instrumental in securing the present terminal. He aided in the enterprise by subscribing liberally to the stock, and was a director and auditor for many years.

He has been twice elected to represent his town in the Legislature, first in 1885, when he was Chairman of the Library Committee, and again in 1886, when he served on the Railroad Committee. He was also a director in the Deep River National Bank for many years, and served at various times as Town Auditor of Accounts, and also as United States Grand Juror. He is a Life Member of the Connecticut Humane Society and of the Acton Library.

While residing in New York he was a member of St Timothy Episcopal Church, and held the office of Treasurer, Vestryman and Warden. On his return to his native town he joined the Grace Episcopal Church and was largely instrumental in the erection of the beautiful stone edifice—its present place of worship, and was one of the most liberal contributors to the building fund. He has been active in church work, and during the past thirty years has held the various offices of Clerk, Treasurer, Vestryman, etc, and later that of Senior Warden.

He married, at Westbrook, Conn, Oct 12, 1851 Emily Maria, daughter of William Stokes, son of Richard, son of Jonathan, Jr, son of Jonathan Stokes, Sen, who came from England with his wife and two children (one of whom was Jonathan, Jr) and settled in Branford Conn.

Jonathan Stokes, Jr, son of Jonathan, was born in England and came with his parents to Branford, Conn. He was a seafaring man and was lost overboard two days out from Boston on his passage to the West Indies. He married Hannah Goodrich, of Branford, and had Jonathan (3), Merriam, Hannah and *Richard*

Richard Stokes, youngest child of Jonathan Jr, and Hannah (Goodrich) Stokes, was born July 2, 1761 2. He served in the War of the Revolution. He was a private in Capt Lay's company, 4th Conn Regiment, commanded by Col Zebulon Butler. His name appears only in a book copied from the rolls of said organization, which shows that he enlisted July 5, 1781, for six months. He married Jerusha, daughter of Daniel Lay, Jr, son of Daniel, son of Robert (3)

*Robert Lay (3), son of Robert (2), was born June 22, 1681. He was an inn keeper. He married Mary, daughter of Daniel Grinnell, whose wife was Lydia Peabody, daughter of William Peabody and Elizabeth Alden, daughter of John Alden of the Mayflower

The children of Richard and Jerusha (Lay) Stokes his wife were

    1   Richard Stokes (2) born Jan 25, 1787

    2   Harry Stokes, born July 4, 1789

    3   John Stokes born Oct 26, 1791

    4   Fanny Stokes, born Oct 21, 1793

    5   *William Stokes*, born May 20, 1796

    6   Eliza Stokes, born May 8, 1798

    7   Charles Stokes, born Nov 7, 1800

    8   Nancy Stokes, born Sept 10, 1804

    9   Edward Stokes, born Feb 20, 1806

William Stokes, fifth child of Richard and Jerusha Stokes, was born in Westbrook, May 20, 1796, died there Nov 9, 1880 He married, in Westbrook Nov 25, 1819, Lydia Kelsey (born in Killingworth May 6 1798, died in Westbrook, Nov 1, 1882) Their children were

I. Eliza Ann, born in Saybrook, Westbrook parish, Aug 23 1820, died there May 12, 1886, married in Westbrook parish, Nov 30, 1843, Dana Bristol Page (born in Cheshire, Conn, Aug 12, 1809, died in Westbrook, Nov 16, 1892)

II   Susan Amelia, born in Westbrook parish, March 12, 1822   Unmarried

III   William Stokes, Jr, born in Westbrook parish, June 2, 1825, died there Sept 25, following

IV   William Stokes (2), born in Westbrook parish, June 25, 1826   Unmarried

V   *Emily Maria*, born in Westbrook parish, Nov 21, 1831, died in Old Saybrook, Oct 5, 1895, she was married in Westbrook, Oct 12, 1851, to Daniel C Spencer

VI   Ellen Gertrude, born in Westbrook parish, July 13 1837   Unmarried

Daniel Chapman Spencer, by his wife Emily Maria (Stokes) Spencer, had issue

I   William David Spencer, born at New Haven, Conn, July 5, 1852

II   Ella Maria Spencer, born in New York City, Nov 4, 1856, married in Old Saybrook, May 10, 1882, Brunswick Wellington Leonard, of St Johns, New Brunswick, died at Saybrook Nov 7, 1900   Their children were

    1   Grace Emily Leonard, born in Old Saybrook, Aug 8, 1883, died same day

    2   Spencer Wellesly Leonard, born in Old Saybrook, Oct 7, 1884

    3   Brunswick Wellesley Leonard, born in Old Saybrook, Aug 10, 1888

    4   Ella Morgan Leonard, born in Old Saybrook, July 1, 1892, died there July 2, 1893

    5   Emily Stokes Leonard, born in Old Saybrook, April 22, 1900   Died Dec 27, 1900

III   Daniel Stokes Spencer, born in New York City Sept 2, 1860, married Dec 1, 1898, Mary Ellen Fish, born in Griswold, Conn, Oct 26, 1872   They have one son, Daniel Fish Spencer, born Dec 8, 1899, in Saybrook

IV   Grace Emily Spencer, born in New York City, Nov 11, 1861, married at Saybrook, June 10, 1891, John Clayton Wood, of New York City, born there Oct 1, 1859

V.   George Jarvis Spencer, born in New York, May 2, 1866, died Nov 10, 1892, in Saybrook

VI   Edmund Chapman Spencer, born in Old Saybrook, Jan 8, 1869, married there Nov 21, 1895, Florence Josephine Burr, born in Cromwell Conn, Oct 21, 1872   They have one son, Clayton Burr, born in Saybrook, Nov 27, 1897

VII   Frederick Clarence Spencer, born at Old Saybrook, March 27, 1870

VIII   Harry Russell Spencer, born at Old Saybrook, July 9, 1875, died there May 5, 1876

HARRIET AMELIA SPENCER, ninth child of David and Rachel (Bushnell) Spencer, was born Dec 21, 1825, died there Jan 9, 1852, married there June 20, 1849, James Smith Eldert   They had one son, James Eldert   He married—no date

EMILY ANN SPENCER, tenth child of David and Rachel (Bushnell) Spencer, was born May 5, 1828, died June 28, 1895, at Lawtey, Florida, married at Saybrook, Sept 12, 1882, Tunis Lynk, of New Lenox, Ill, no issue

MARY AUGUSTA SPENCER, eleventh and youngest child of David and Rachel (Bushnell) Spencer, was born in Saybrook, Aug 10, 1832, died in New York City, Oct 11, 1900, married in New York City, Jan 18, 1854, Hiram Fuller Phelps (born Nov 15, 1829, died Aug 11, 1891) They had issue

I   Edward Fuller Phelps, born Oct 20, 1854, married 1884, Justina Brecker   They had Arthur Phelps, Edward Phelps, Fredrick Phelps, Grace Phelps   Married, second, Anna Margaret Muller, of Philadelphia, Pa, Nov 19, 1900

II   Alvin Spencer Phelps, born Feb 12, 1856

III   Antoinette Flora Phelps, born Nov 26, 1857, married Sept 3, 1885, William Frank Harrison   They had issue, Charles William Harrison, born July 20, 1886, in East Haddam, and Russell Spencer Harrison, born in East Haddam, Dec 2, 1888

IV   Mary Willey Phelps, born June 23, 1859.

V   Emily Maria Phelps, born Dec 12, 1860, died Sept 21, 1863

VI   Susan Chalker Phelps, born March 5, 1862

VII   Hiram Lincoln Phelps, born May 16, 1863, married to Theresa De Bear, Nov 16, 1895   They had Albert Phelps, Lilian Phelps

VIII   Maria Parker Phelps, born June 25, 1864; married Nov 16, 1893, Albert Kummer They had Viola Kummer, born Nov 16, 1895, and Daisy Kummer, born May 31, 1897, died November, 1899

IX   Robert Phelps, born Aug. 3, 1865, died Sept 21, 1865

X   Albert David Phelps, born Aug 15, 1866; died April 22, 1886.

XI   Ernest Mortimer Phelps, born Oct 10, 1868, married May, 1892, Rose Kelwig   They had a son, Vernon Scheile, born April, 1895, in Hadlyme

XII   Julia Ann Phelps, born Nov 24, 1870, died Dec 29, 1887

XIII   George Phelps, born May 10, 1873, died May 12, 1873

XIV.   Walter Chapman Phelps, born May 5, 1874

XV.   Harriet Amelia Phelps, born January 6, 1876; died March 28, 1892.

DESCENDANTS OF GEORGE SPENCER, FOURTH CHILD OF JOSEPH (2) (SEE PAGE 61) AND LUCY (POST)
SPENCER, SON OF JOSEPH (1), SON OF CALEB, SON OF THOMAS, SON OF GERRARD SPENCER

George Spencer, seventh child of Joseph (2) and fourth child by his second wife, Lucy
(Post) Spencer, was born Oct. 6, 1787. At an early age he was apprenticed to Nathan Pratt, of
Essex, Conn., then engaged in the jewelry business. He served as a private in the War of
1812. He removed to Deep River in 1818, having previously, with others, formed a copartnership with Ezra Williams & Co., manufacturers of ivory combs, etc. This continued until 1830,
when it was succeeded by George Read & Co., and in 1864 became a joint stock company.

Mr. Spencer was deacon of the Congregational Church of Deep River from its organization
in 1834 till his death, July 24, 1878. He was President of the Deep River Bank from Nov. 1850,
to January, 1865, when he resigned. He was succeeded by Henry Wooster, who died August
1866. It was said by a cotemporary he was a man of robust mind, incorruptible integrity,
and strong religious convictions, and though nearly 91 years old when he died, his mental
faculties were preserved in a good degree of vigor until the last. [Hist. Middlesex Co., p. 557.]
On the Sunday following his funeral his pastor, Rev. W. H. Knouse, delivered a memorial sermon as a tribute to his christian character and exemplary life.

He married 1st, Julia Pratt, born Oct. 24, 1755, daughter of Comfort and Susannah (Tiley)
Pratt, Sept. 12, 1813. She died March 29, 1845.

The lineage of Julia Pratt has been traced to Thomas and Joan Pratt, of Baldock, Hertfordshire, England (1539), through his son Andrew Pratt, father of Rev. William Pratt, born
in 1567, for thirty years prior to his death in 1629 Rector of the parish of Stevenage, near Baldock Hertfordshire. His son William, known as Lieut. William Pratt, came to Newtown
(Cambridge) in 1632 or 1633, removed to Hartford in 1636 and from there to that part of
the original town of Saybrook known as Potapaug in 1645, being among the first settlers
there. His wife was Elizabeth Clark, and from them was descended in direct line. 1 Nathaniel Pratt, born about 1660 or 1661; married Sarah Beamont, May 2, 1688. 2 Deacon Hezekiah Pratt, born July 9, 1701; married a lady whose christian name was Ann, died Oct. 4,
1786. 3 Comfort, born in 1746, married Susannah Tiley, June 4, 1774, and died Feb. 19, 1778.
[Pratt Family, by Rev. F. W. Chapman.]

He married 2nd, Ursula Read, born April 23, 1789, daughter of Cornelius and Temperance
(Williams) Read Oct. 20, 1845, who died March 27, 1853.

Third, Ann E. Bates, daughter of Barnabas and Rebecca (Clark) Bates, Jan. 4, 1854; died
Sept. 17, 1882.

George Spencer died July 24, 1878.

Deacon George Spencer, by his wife Julia (Pratt) Spencer, had issue :

I   GEORGE TILEY SPENCER, born Nov. 6, 1814, residence Corning, N. Y. See record

II   Julia Spencer, born Sept. 2, 1817; died Feb. 15, 1819

III RICHARD PRATT SPENCER, born Feb. 12, 1820. See record

IV Julia Minerva Spencer, 2nd, born Nov 27, 1822 , married Dr. Ambrose Pratt, of Deep River, son of Ambrose and Polly (Southworth) Pratt

V Jane Elizabeth Spencer, born Feb 23, 1825 , married John W Marvin

VI Susan Augusta Spencer, born Feb 16, 1829 ; married to Rev Charles H Bullard, of Hartford Conn

I **Kon. George Tiley Spencer,** eldest child of George and Julia (Pratt) Spencer, was born Nov 6, 1814, in that part of the original town of Saybrook, Conn , now Essex, and included what at an early day was known as Potapaug Quarter

He was prepared for college at Amherst Academy, Mass , Westfield Academy, Mass , and Hopkins Grammar School, New Haven, and graduated from Yale College in the class of 1837

Mr Spencer began his legal studies in 1839, in the office of Governor Eilsworth, at Hartford, Conn , and was subsequently a student with John G Forbes, of Syracuse, N Y , and was admitted to the bar in July, 1841 In August of the same year he began the practice of law in Corning, N Y , where he has since resided He was identified with the old Whig party until it ceased to exist, and was among the first to join the Republican party after its formation He was elected to the State Legislature of New York of 1857, and served as a member of the Judiciary Committee He was a member of the Constitutional Convention of 1867 He was elected Judge of Steuben County for the term commencing in 1872, continuing in office until 1878 He continued in the active practice of his profession until 1896, retiring at the age of 80 He has been engaged with his brother, R P Spencer, of Deep River, Conn , for many years in the collection of matters relating to the history and genealogy of the Spencer family

He married, Nov 3 1842, Harriet Stacy, daughter of Ira and Roxanna (Glover) Stacy, of Belchertown, Mass

Roxanna Glover was a descendant of Capt John Glover, son of Thomas and Margery (Deane) Glover, of the parish of Rumhill, in Prescott, Lancashire, England, where he was born Aug 12, 1600, and Anna his wife He was one of the 'London Company,' organized for the purpose of settlement in New England, on the shores of which he arrived in the *Mary and John* May 31,1630, and settled in Dorchester, where, and in Boston, he was a prominent man of affairs He died Feb 11, 1653 The line of descent is as follows .

1 Rev Pelatiah Glover, son of Capt John and Anna (————) Glover, born in Dorchester in Nov 1636 , died at Springfield, March 24, 1692 He married, May 20, 1660, Hannah Cullick, daughter of Capt John Cullick

2 Pelatiah Glover, son of Rev Pelatiah and Hannah (Cullick) Glover, born at Springfield, Jan 27, 1665 6 , died there April 1, 1739 He married, Jan 7, 1686, Hannah Parsons, daughter of Joseph and Mary (Bliss) Parsons, of Northampton

3 Samuel Glover, son of Pelatiah and Hannah (Parsons) Glover, born in Springfield, Dec 16, 1706 , married Dec 14, 1749, Joyce (Newcomb) Jones, widow The date of his death is not known

4 John Glover, son of Samuel and Joyce (Newcomb Jones) Glover, born in Wilbraham,

Mass,. May 3, 1753, and died there July 21, 1830 He married in 1778, Mercy Colton, daughter of Benjamin and Mercy Colton, of Springfield

5 Roxana Glover, daughter of John and Mercy (Colton) Glover, born Dec 1, 1788; married Jan 10, 1810, [Family Bible] Ira Stacy, son of Mark and Julia (Root) Stacy, born May 9, 1788, died May 20, 1838

Children of Ira and Roxana (Glover) Stacy

1   John, born June 15, 1810, died about 1888 married Betsey Matilda Doolittle, daughter of Hon Mark and Betsey Matilda (Smith) Doolittle, of Belchertown, Nov 28, 1838, graduate of Yale College 1837, had John, born May 27, 1841, died in early infancy, Sarah Doolittle, born May 28, 1843 died Sept 25, 1843

2   Ira, born Sept 6, 1815, died June 9, 1827

3   *Harriet*, born June 3, 1821, wife of George T Spencer, died May 7, 1897

4   Samuel, born May 27, 1827, married Terissa Giles in 1857, died Oct 24, 1857

Roxana (Glover) Stacy married 2nd, James Miller, of Williamsburg, Mass, died at Corning, N Y, Aug 25, 1877

George T Spencer, by his wife Harriet (Stacy) Spencer, had issue

1   Ellen Julia, born June 9, 1844, died April 1849

2   Roxana Jane, born March 9, 1846, died July 1, 1846

3   George Stacy, born March 17 1847 He served with honor to himself and his country in the War of the Rebellion, enlisting as private in the 10th N Y Cavalry in March, 1864, and serving until the close of the war, and was commissioned 2nd Lieutenant In 1872 he graduated from Albany Law School and soon after engaged in the drug business at St Cloud, Minnesota, where he has since resided

He married 1st, Martha Macomber, June 20, 1876, who died Jan 31, 1880, married 2nd, Jane Augusta Piatt, June 28, 1883, daughter of Dr Ambrose and Julia Minerva (Spencer) Piatt, of Chester, Conn

Children by his first wife

George T Spencer, born April 6, 1877, died June 13, 1893

Herbert Spencer, born June 8, 1879, died Feb 3, 1880

Children by second wife

Ambrose Piatt Spencer, born Jan 31, 1885

Hugh Spencer, born July 13, 1887

Gerald Spencer, born Oct 23, 1891

4   Harriet Augusta born March 1, 1849, graduated at Elmira Female College She married Horace N Pond (born July 31, 1843) Oct 20, 1869, at that time cashier of J N Hungerford's Bank, Corning, subsequently in business at Elmira and afterwards at Boston, residing in Dorchester While there he prepared for and entered the Ministry of the Presbyterian Church, removed to Nebraska, and, after a residence of some years in that State, to Kansas His pres-

ent residence is Topeka He was compelled several years since to abandon ministerial labors on account of deafness Their children were,

    1   Kate Williams Pond. born May 27, 1872, died May 16, 1876

    2   Robert Spencer Pond born July 19, 1876, graduate of Washburn College, Topeka, 1890, now (1901) Professor of Mathematics in Pendleton Academy, Pendleton, Oregon

    3   Horace Philip Pond born Feb 10 1882

    5. Emma Roxana, born April 9, 1851, married Aug 25, 1873, Rev Albert W Hubbard He graduated at Amherst College 1867, and from Princeton Theological Seminary 1870 They immediately sailed for Sivas, Turkey, as missionaries, where they continued to reside until his death, with the exception of two visits to this country, and where she still resides (1900) Their eight children, all born at Sivas, are Ray Spencer, born Dec 31, 1875, Lew Crescens, born Sept 1, 1877, both graduates of Amherst College, 1900, Faith, born April 14, 1880, Chauncey, born Feb 26, 1882, George, born Feb 26, 1882, Hugh, born March 19, 1887, Mary, born Feb 2, 1890, Theodore Horace, born July 5, 1892 Mr Hubbard died at Sivas, April 25, 1899, greatly lamented by all classes of the population

    6   John, born January 15, 1855, died May 21, 1857

    7   Betsey, born Oct 31, 1859, graduated at Wellesley College in 1883, afterwards became Preceptress of Corning Free Academy, which position she resigned in 1897 She married Frederick William Kriger, of Waite & Kriger, merchants of Corning, Aug 31, 1898 They had issue Frederick Spencer Kriger, born Sept. 16, 1899, Ralph Stacy King, Jan 7, 1901

    8   Richard, born July 27, 1861, died July 18, 1862

    9   Hugh Spencer, born Jan 6, 1864, graduate of Corning Free Academy in 1882, having been awarded the Olcott prize consisting of a gold medal of the value of about ten dollars, from the income of a fund given to the Trustees of the Academy by Hon Alexander Olcott, for the best scholarship. He entered Yale College in 1884, but was compelled to leave at the end of the college year by reason of ill health, which developed into a slowly wasting disease of which he died Jan 14, 1889

    10   Clarissa, born Jan 6, 1864, married Sept 4, 1892, Harry H Pratt, of Corning, by whom she has five children George Wollage and Sophia, born June 23, 1893, Hugh Spencer, born July 16, 1894, Harriet, born Nov 3, 1895, Ransom. born Dec 9, 1899

    III **Hon. Richard Pratt Spencer,** third child of Deacon George and Julia (Pratt) Spencer, was born in Deep River, Conn, Feb 12, 1820 His knowledge of the rudimentary branches of education was obtained at the village school, and he was afterwards sent to Madison, Berlin, Conn, and Belchertown, Mass high schools Being thus fully equipped for a business career, he entered the employ of his father's firm and soon after attaining his majority joined the firm as a partner Later he organized the firm of Pratt, Spencer & Co, with Ulysses and Alexis Pratt as partners This firm engaged largely in the manufacture of ivory turnings and ivory piano keys He sold his interest in the business in 1850 and removed to Corning, N Y, and

there established a banking business which he carried on successfully for several years He returned to his native town in 1866 and was shortly after elected President of the Deep River National Bank, which position he still occupies

Naturally of a retiring disposition, Mr Spencer has been but little in public life He gave his hearty support to the cause of the Union during the Civil War and has been identified with the Republican party since its organization, having been formerly connected with the old Whig party He was elected to the State Senate in 1882-3, and served as Chairman of the Committee on Fisheries, and during the second session was Chairman of the Committee on Banks He was two years treasurer of the Deep River Savings Bank an institution in which he has always taken a deep interest He has added much to the wealth and prosperity of the town, and his picturesque home near the banks of the Connecticut is said to be one of the finest residences in the State

Mr Spencer married 1st, in 1850, Clarissa, daughter of George H Chapman and Lucia (Tulley) Chapman, of Old Saybrook She died Dec 16, 1871, without issue He married 2nd, Feb 28, 1887, Julianna, daughter of Richard Lynde Selden, of Hadlyme, son of Richard Ely Selden (2), son of Richard Ely Selden (1), son of Col Samuel, son of Samuel, son of Joseph, son of Thomas, the ancestor

Thomas Selden, the ancestor was one of the founders of Hartford, Conn , in 1639 , was admitted freeman 1640 By his wife, Esther ——, he had, Thomas, bap Aug 31, 1645 , John, died May, 1650 , Mary, born March 26, 1648 , Esther, born March 3, 1650, died next year , *Joseph*, born Nov 2, 1651 , Hannah Sarah He died before the end of 1655 His will names widow Esther, who married Andrew Warner

Joseph Selden, son of Thomas and Esther (———) Selden, was born Nov 2, 1651, at Hartford, Conn He removed first to Hadley, Mass , thence to Deerfield, back to Hadley again, and finally to Lyme, Conn , and there purchased a large estate partly in Haddam He died before February 1725 He married Rebecca Church, of Hatfield, daughter of Dea Edward Church, son of Richard Church, of Hartford

Richard Church, of Hartford, 1637, "an original proprietor," says Savage, "whose first residence is unknown, removed about 1660 to Hadley '

Colturn says "As nearly as can now be traced he was an uncle of Col Benjamin Church, who commanded the party which killed King Philip in 1676, and who was sent on an expedition against the eastern Indians of New England in 1704, and did them and the French much damage He removed to Hartford with Hooker's congregation in 1636 "

His widow, Ann, died 10 March, 1684, aged 83, and in his will only four children are named These were, *Edward*, John, Mary and Samuel, all probably born in England

Dea Edward Church, son of Richard Church, of Hartford, was born in England, 1628, and had perhaps been some time at New Haven He removed to Hartford and was then deacon His children were Mary married Philip Russell as his third wife , *Rebecca*, married 1697 Joseph Selden ; Hepzebah, married 16 Sept 1696, Samuel Spencer

Joseph Selden, by his wife Rebecca (Church) Selden, had Rebecca, born 1678, Esther, 1680,

R P Spencer

Eng'd by H.B.Hall sons New York

died soon, Joseph, 1682; Thomas, 1684, Hannah, Mary, March 5, 1689, Esther again; *Samuel*, born May 17, 1695

Samuel Selden, youngest child of Joseph and Rebecca (Church) Selden, was born May 17, 1695 He married Deborah Dudley They had two sons, Samuel 'the Colonel, and Ezra "the Squire "

Colonel Samuel Selden, son of Samuel and Deborah (Dudley) Selden, was born at Hadlyme, Jan 11, 1723 He served in a military capacity before the Revolution, as appears by the following, Conn Colonial Records, 1771

"This Assembly do appoint Samuel Selden, Esq, to be Major of the third regiment of militia in this Colony '

Immediately after the breaking out of the War of the Revolution he offered his services to the State in response to a call from the Assembly, and was commissioned Colonel of the Fourth Battalion, Wadsworth's Brigade Johnston, in his description of the Battle of Long Island says

"Another of those citizen soldiers who came from the substantial element in the population was Colonel Selden A descendant of the Seldens who were among the first settlers in the Connecticut Valley, fifty years of age, possessing a large estate incapacitated for severe military duty, the father of twelve children, he nevertheless answered the Governor's call for troops and joined the army at New York, from which he was destined not to return '

He took an active part in the Battle of Long Island, Aug 27, 1776, and when the American army retreated from New York, Sept 15, he, with many others, was captured Johnston, in describing the "Kip's Bay ' affair, says During these scenes Wadsworth's and Scott's brigades, which were below Douglass on the river lines, saw that their only safety lay, also, in immediate retreat, and falling back they joined the other brigades above, though not without suffering some loss ' Col Selden was confined in the prison in the east side of the City Hall Park, now used as the Register's Office, where he died of fever 'on Friday P M, October 11, about 3 o'clock " In the latter part of his sickness he was attended by Dr Thatcher, a British surgeon, who paid him every attention He was buried in the Brick Church-yard (Presbyterian) He married Elizabeth Ely, daughter of Richard Ely and Elizabeth Peck, of Lyme They had issue Richard Ely Selden and others

Richard Ely Selden, son of Col Samuel and Elizabeth (Ely) Selden, was born at Hadlyme, in 1759, died 23 January, 1848, aged 89 He married Desire Colt, daughter of Joseph Colt and Desire Pratt, of Saybrook, Conn They had seven children, of whom Richard Ely Selden, Jr, was the sixth

Richard Ely Selden (2), son of Richard Ely Selden (1) and Desire Colt, was born in Hadlyme, June 13, 1797 Graduated from Yale College in 1818; died March 3, 1868 He married 21 Feb 1821, Eliza Lynde (born 5 Feb 1796), daughter of William Lynde, Esq, and Sally Kirtland, his wife; she died 23 Jan 1866

Richard Lynde Selden, son of Richard Ely Selden (2) and Eliza (Lynde) Selden, was born in Hadlyme, Oct 23, 1824, married in Higganum, Conn, 22 May, 1851, Sarah M Loper, daugh-

ter of Rev Stephen A Loper and Sarah B Meigs, his wife, of Madison, Conn   They had, among other children, *Julianna*

Julianna Selden, eldest child of Richard Lynde and Sarah (Loper) Selden, was born in Higganum, Conn , 22 Feb 1852   She was married Feb 22, 1877, to Richard P Spencer

Richard P Spencer, by his wife Julianna (Selden) Spencer, had issue

1   Richard Selden Spencer, born 15 February, 1878 , entered Yale College 1897

2   Florence Elizabeth Spencer, born 29 February, 1880

3   George Selden Spencer, born 27 May, 1884

IV   JULIA MINERVA SPENCER, fourth child of Dea George Spencer, born Nov 27, 1822 , married Nov 17, 1844, Dr Ambrose Pratt, son of Ambrose and Dolly (Southworth) Pratt, born July 11, 1814, a descendant of Lieut William Pratt, the settler. Dr Pratt was a graduate of Yale College in the class of 1837, and of Columbia Medical College, Washington, D C , in 1843, in which year he commenced practice in Chester, Conn where he continued to reside till his death, July 11, 1891, except about five years residence in Milwaukee, Wis He served in the Civil War as surgeon of the 22d Regiment Connecticut Volunteers, from Nov 1862, to July, 1863, when the enlistment of the regiment expired [See Pratt Family]

Children .

1   Ella Starkey, born March 15, 1846 , married Nov 5 1871, Charles D Fitch

2   Julia Cornelia, born March 2, 1848 , died Feb 26, 1849

3   Jane Augusta, born Nov 8, 1852 , married June 28, 1883, George S Spencer, of St Cloud, Minn

4   Hattie, born Feb 24, 1857

5   Clara Bradley, born Dec 7, 1859

V   JANE ELIZABETH, fifth child of Dea George and Julia (Pratt) Spencer, born Feb 23, 1825 , married Nov 27, 1845, John W. Marvin, of Deep River, son of Deacon John Marvin, born at Lyme, Jan 12, 1824   Besides having held various town offices and being a director or trustee in moneyed and other corporations, he was, in 1871 and 1872, a member of the popular branch of the Connecticut Legislature from Saybrook, and in 1886 Senator from the 21st Senatorial District   Mr Marvin died January 2, 1896.

Children .

1   Julia Spencer, born Nov 4, 1848 ; died Sept. 4, 1875

2   George Selden, born June 3, 1851 ; married Augusta Pratt, daughter of Milton and Penniah (Todd) Pratt, May 22, 1879 She was born May 10, 1855. They have one child, Charles Arthur Marvin, born Aug 12, 1883

3   Charles Reynold, born Jan 26, 1856 , married June 5, 1889, Harriet Aurelia Lord, daughter of Joseph and Alice G (Fleetham) Lord, who was born May 23, 1866.

Children ·

John Kimball Lord, born June 8, 1890

Harry B Lord, born Aug 29, 1891.

Alice Fleetham Lord, born Dec 17, 1893

Julia Augusta Lord, born Feb 11, 1899

Lydia Jane Lord, born April 30, 1900

VI   SUSAN AUGUSTA sixth child of Dea George and Julia (Pratt) Spencer, born Feb 16, 1829, married Rev Charles Henry Bullard Oct 14, 1852, died Aug 7, 1896

Mr Bullard, born at Uxbridge, Mass , Feb 13, 1820, was the son of Luther Bullard, born at Uxbridge, Dec 3, 1788, and Hannah (Dudley) Bullard, born at Oxford, Mass , Nov 19, 1794, who were married Dec 8, 1814   He graduated at Yale College in 1847, and Yale Theological Seminary in 1852 was pastor of the Congregational church in Rockville, Conn , from 1852 to 1857 removed from there to Hartford, where he resided until his death   He was successively District Secretary of American (Boston) Tract Society, State Missionary for Connecticut Home Missionary Society, and District Secretary of American (N Y) Tract Society, his labors in the last named capacity terminating in 1895   He died Oct 15, 1897

Children

1   Clara Louise, born Oct 15 1853 , died April 6 1856

2   Arthur Edward, born July 16, 1856 , died April 29, 1863

3   Alice, born Feb 28, 1858 , married Rev Arthur Fessenden Skeel March 27, 1884, by whom she has children Marion Spencer born April 12, 1885 , Elizabeth Blodgett born Oct 12, 1890 Katharine Anna born July, 1896

4   Anna White, born June 21, 1860

5   Mary Agnes born Nov 23 1862, died Feb 28, 1871

6   Herbert Spencer, born May 19, 1865 He is a lawyer located in Hartford

DESCENDANTS OF CALEB SPENCER (2), SON OF CALEB (1), SON OF THOMAS, SON OF GERRARD

Caleb Spencer (2,) brother of Joseph and third child of Caleb (1) and Hannah (———) Spencer, was born in Westbrook parish (then a part of the town of Saybrook, now the town of Westbrook) Dec 8, 1724 It is quite probable that he served in the Revolutionary War, as "Connecticut Men in the Revolution" contains the name of Caleb Spencer, who served as corporal in Capt Uriah Seymour's company, Major Sheldon's Regiment of Light Horse Caleb (2) died Sept 30, 1783 His wife was Mrs Hannah Stokes (née Goodrich), widow of Richard Stokes (see Stokes Family, following that of D C Spencer, page 71) She died Dec 29, 1791, and was buried in Westbrook, where the inscription on her tombstone is still clear and distinct (Quite an imposing monument to her memory was erected in Branford by the Goodrich family who were probably not aware of the fact that she was buried in Westbrook) The children of this marriage were Caleb (2) the eldest, who died unmarried, *Timothy*, born 1772, and John, who went West with his family about 1820

CAPT TIMOTHY SPENCER second child of Caleb (2) and Hannah (Stokes, née Goodrich) Spencer was born in Westbrook, Conn , 1772   Like many young men of that period residing along the coast towns of Connecticut he was a ship carpenter and ship builder, and almost every man in that section of country was directly or indirectly interested in shipping and ship building This environment developed a class of seafaring men—bold, intelligent, hardy—who proved an

honor to our merchant marine service, second to no other nation. Capt Timothy Spencer encouraged that spirit of independence and manhood in his children and laid the foundation of their successful career as navigators and shipping merchants. He married Polly Bushnell (born 1783) daughter of Jordan and Sarah (Piatt) Bushnell. Sarah Piatt, the wife of Jordan Bushnell, was the daughter of Timothy Piatt and Sarah Parker son of Isaac Piatt, son of Ensign John Piatt, eldest son of Lieut. William Piatt, one of the chief founders of Saybrook and one of the most important men in the colony of Connecticut. (See Piatt Family, page   ) Jordan Bushnell, above referred to, served in the War of the Revolution as private in Capt Martin Kirtland's Company Col Erastus Wolcott's Regiment (soon after Brigadier General and later Governor of Conn) This company was stationed at New London, Conn Feb 28, '77, and was made up principally of Saybrook men

Capt Timothy Spencer by his wife Polly (Bushnell) Spencer had issue

  I Margette, born Feb 29, 1806
  II Emeline, born Aug 28, 1807
  III Frederick W born Jan 7, 1810
  IV JOSEPH WHITTLESEY, born June 12, 1812
  V ALFRED GOODRICH, born July 9, 1814
  VI Eloise, born Oct 8, 1816
  VII Harriet E , born July 10, 1820

Capt. Joseph Whittlesey Spencer, fourth child of Timothy and Polly (Bushnell) Spencer, was born at Westbrook, Conn , June 16th 1812 With a natural taste for a seafaring life, he engaged as a boy in the coasting trade on Long Island Sound until, at the age of sixteen, he shipped as an ordinary seaman on the "Athenian" and made his first deep water voyage to Carthagena Later, while on a voyage to Cuba, the captain and most of the crew being taken sick with yellow fever, the mate took charge of the ship and young Spencer was made second mate He soon rose to the position of first mate and in 1834 was placed in command of the brig "Medina"

Two years later he made his first whaling voyage as captain of the barque "General Brown," and managed one of the boats which captured the first whale His share in the profits of this voyage enabled him to purchase an interest in the "Crusoe" Later he built and commanded the "Rose Standish," and in 1848 he built the "William Rathbone" With this vessel, which was nearly three times the tonnage of the former one, he entered into the Liverpool trade

Among the achievements of Captain Spencer's life, one which added greatly to his reputation among seafaring men, was the building of the "David Crockett, one of the most famous, as well as one of the largest and fastest of that class of clipper ships which made the American merchant marine famous This remarkably successful vessel he commanded for four years and then gave up active service on the sea

His ship continued in the California trade, making an enviable record for short passages and financial success until the American wooden ship was displaced by the iron ships built and

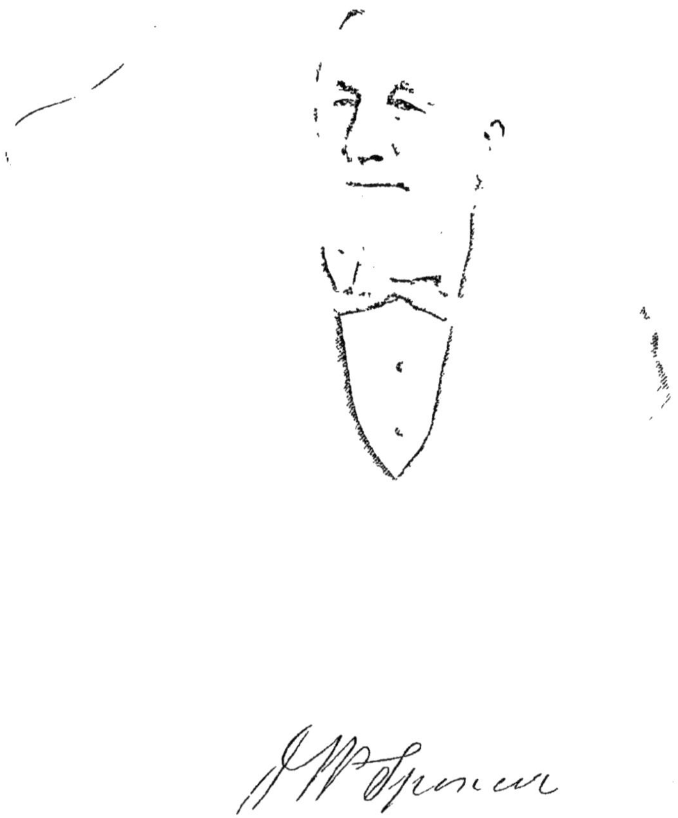

owned abroad. After this the "David Crockett" suffered the fate of her sister ships by being converted into a coal barge. For many years she continued in this service until in the latter part of the year 1898 she made her last port and ran aground on Romer shoal at the entrance of New York harbor. All through the winter she lay there in the sight of all the incoming and outgoing shipping, a sad monument to the memory of the American clipper ship of days gone by.

Captain Spencer, having left the sea, in 1855, became manager, joint owner and adviser of all the shipping interests controlled by Lawrence Giles & Co., of New York City. He continued in this position for several years until (owing to our unfortunate navigation laws) the shipping interests of this country gradually fell into the hands of foreigners and ceased to be profitable to American ship owners. He then retired to his beautiful home in Westbrook, Conn., where he resided most of his time during the remainder of his life. He died May 23, 1900, at the ripe old age of 88.

Capt. Spencer was one of the best known and most popular sea captains that ever sailed out of the port of New York. Fearless in the discharge of his duty, the very soul of honor and integrity, he led an upright, blameless life, and was a worthy representative of that noble band of American sea captains of half a century ago, who reflected honor and glory on the flag under which they sailed.

Capt. Spencer married (Sept. 2, 1838,) Amelia A., daughter of John Stokes, son of Richard.

Richard Stokes the son of Jonathan, has already been referred to on page 71. The *Eastern State Journal* furnishes the following additional data relative to his service in the Revolution.

"During the Revolution while General Washington made his headquarters at White Plains, he selected some five or six trusty men to execute a dangerous commission. Among the number was a young volunteer, Richard Stokes, of Westbrook, Connecticut. His earnestness, courage and enthusiasm had won the respect of Washington, who asked him if he felt ready to engage in a perilous but necessary undertaking. Stokes promptly replied that he was ready to serve his country at all hazards. The General then gave them their instructions and the party started forthwith, proceeding cautiously through the woods and keeping well out of sight until they reached New York City. Here, favored by the darkness of a cloudy night, they appropriated one of the enemy's boats, and, with muffled oars, glided down the river to Staten Island, passing directly under the enemy's guns without being discovered. Here they received a large sum of money—a treasure which the close blockade of the British squadron had hitherto prevented from reaching its destination—a treasure sent over from France by those noble friends of liberty who were ever ready to aid us, even with their lives, in our struggles for freedom. The brave little party then returned as they had gone, and arriving safely, delivered the treasure to their General. Soon after this occurred the battle of White Plains, in which this brave youth again served his country in a manner none the less hazardous and honorable. Mr. Stokes enlisted at the beginning of the war and served faithfully to its close. Often, after the fatigue of a long march, had he and his comrades lain down in the woods to rest, and awoke to find a heavy sheet of snow for their coverlet. At the close of the war Mr. Stokes returned to his Connecticut home, where many of his descendants now reside."

Capt Joseph Whittlesey Spencer by his wife, Amelia (Stokes) Spencer, had issue

   I JOSEPH TIMOTHY, born Aug 23 1842 (See record)

  II JAMES HICKS, born Sept 16, 1845 (See record)

 III Aribella Maria, born Jan 24, 1848, died Oct , 1875

 IV Winfield Scott, born March 7, 1850 (See record)

  V John Stokes born Aug 20 1852, married Annie Abbott

CAPT JOSEPH TIMOTHY SPENCER, eldest child of Capt Joseph Whittlesey Spencer and his wife, Amelia Stokes, was born Aug 23, 1842 At an early age he followed in the footsteps of his father and adopted a seafaring life   His first voyage was made in the " David Crockett " At the breaking out of the Civil War he entered the transport service and was appointed captain of the steamer " Haze ' After the close of the war he returned to the merchant service and became connected with the Galveston (Texas) trade, in which he continued for several years until his death, Oct 20, 1870, being lost at sea by the foundering of his steamer in a hurricane off the Florida coast

He married, Jan 12, 1870 Georgia Rossiter, of Clinton Conn , but had no issue

JAMES HICKS SPENCER, second child of Captain Joseph W and Amelia Stokes Spencer, was born in Westbrook Conn Sept 16, 1845 He attended a select school in New Haven, Conn , where he received a thorough education in those branches best adapted to fit him for a mercantile career He came to New York City in 1863 and entered the house of Lawrence Giles & Co , of which his father was a member He remained with this firm ten years, and in 1874 started in business for himself as an importer principally of shell nuts from the Mediterranean With a constantly increasing trade he is now one of the largest importers in this special line

Outside of business his interest has centered chiefly in military affairs April 7, 1865, he joined the 37th Regiment as private in Company F This was one of the city regiments organized for special service or emergency during the war His company was consolidated with the 9th Regiment and Mr Spencer was made sergeant of Company K Afterwards he became 1st Lieutenant in the 4th Reg N G , S N Y , and in 1872 he was commissioned Captain of Company A, 1st Regiment, N G , S N Y , continuing in this capacity until Dec 27, 1874 when he resigned During this period he took part in all the principal affairs of his regiment He is a life member of the several Masonic bodies, including that of Mecca Temple, Nobles of the Mystic Shrine

He married, July 25, 1876, Alice F Brown, daughter of John Brown, of Albany, N Y , and Mary Ferris, his wife of Boston Their children are Alice Estelle, born June 24, 1877 , Joseph Whittlesey, born Feb 24, 1880, Alice Gertrude born March 20, 1885

WINFIELD SCOTT SPENCER, fourth child of Captain Joseph Whittlesey Spencer and his wife, Amelia (Stokes) Spencer, was born at Westbrook, March 7, 1850 He was educated at the public school and after completing his studies entered the dry goods trade He carried on business for himself at New Rochelle, N Y , for about fifteen years, retiring in Oct , 1900 He married Sarah Isabelle Parrish, of Grand Rapids, Mich , Dec 20 1882

CPSIA information can be obtained
at www.ICGtesting.com
Printed in the USA
LVHW080358051022
730013LV00004B/20